# Listening
## in the
# DARK

**Women Reclaiming the Power of Intuition**

## Also by Amber Tamblyn

US POET LAUREATE
**ADA**
**LIMÓN**

**AMY**
**POEHLER**

**AMERICA**
**FERRERA**

CONGRESSWOMAN
**AYANNA**
**PRESSLEY**

**JIA**
**TOLENTINO**

**SAMANTHA**
**IRBY**

DR. MINDY
**NETTIFEE**

**LIDIA**
**YUKNAVITCH**

# Listening
## in the
# DARK

### Women Reclaiming the Power of Intuition

DR. DARA
**KASS**

**BONNIE**
**TAMBLYN**

**MEREDITH**
**TALUSAN**

DR. NICOLE
**APELIAN**

**HUMA**
**ABEDIN**

**EMILY**
**WELLS**

**JESSICA**
**VALENTI**

# AMBER TAMBLYN

PARK
ROW
BOOKS

PARK
ROW™
BOOKS™

Recycling programs
for this product may
not exist in your area.

ISBN-13: 978-0-7783-3333-3

Listening in the Dark: Women Reclaiming the Power of Intuition

Park Row Books
22 Adelaide St. West, 41st Floor
Toronto, Ontario M5H 4E3, Canada
ParkRowBooks.com
BookClubbish.com

**Printed in U.S.A.**

For the next generation of Knowers:
Ella, Graeme, Zora, Lucia, Mae, Xochi, Lennox, Nyla
and my Marlow.

And for Jack Hirschman.

# TABLE OF CONTENTS

*What is it like to be a woman listening in the dark?*

—Anne Carson

# The Body Always Knows First: An Introduction

*By Amber Tamblyn*

In the dark, my arms reach toward the sky to hold on to someone who is already gone.

Asleep in my bed, the sudden jolt of my body prompted by a dream that left as quickly as it came awoke me before my alarm could. I found my arms outstretched, my fingers casting shadows in the moonlight like wind-spanked branches. Once oriented, I yanked my limbs back close to my chest, gasping, and held myself close. Moments later, my alarm buzzed. I turned it off and reached for my digital watch to check the time and prepare for an early day of work.

The watch has a comforting feature whereby different pictures can be programmed to appear at random each time you look at it. I had been in Toronto, Canada, far away from home for close to six months, so I set the watch with various photos of memories that would sustain me while I was away: my mother on the beach in Santa Monica holding on to her windblown hat, laughing. Our ailing, old dog licking our three-year-old daughter Marlow's face. A trip with friends to a cabin in the woods. My husband drinking his favorite pint of beer at our favorite local bar. That one Beyoncé concert. I loved not knowing which memory awaited me each time I looked at the watch, and each picture's reveal was a welcome surprise that made me feel closer to home.

The watch lit up the blackened room as I looked at its face, and the glow of a picture struck me so bright and so present, I winced: my writing mentor, the poet Jack Hirschman, standing in Caffe Trieste in San Francisco some years earlier, holding my then baby daughter in his arms. She is clutching on to his black shirt with her tiny fingers as his hand cups her diaper, holding her close. Jack is a brilliant writer and has authored more than a hundred books in ten languages as a celebrated poet the world over. In the picture, I can make out the wise rings of his skin, an ancient tree of a man. I can see the rubbed reddish-pink flesh between his thumb and index finger, the place where his pen has rested and written for more than seven decades. His ring finger pushes down against Marlow's diaper, keeping her steady against his chest like a pianist holding a vital note to finish the chord. In the picture, Jack is wearing his signature red suspenders, and silver writing glasses sit on top of his head. His white hair billows down over the canyons of his neck like fog. Marlow is looking out, eyes wide open, and Jack is looking down at her, his massive mustache spread broad across his face from a smile breaching beneath it, the cracks around his eyes deepened with joy.

I held the watch there in the dark room and stared at

the image of them together, unable to get out of bed just yet. My body wouldn't let me. Jack is my creative father, the man who published my first poem at the age of twelve, who taught me everything I know about the power of my emotions put to pen.

"Hey," my husband said, finally stirring in bed next to me. "You better get up and get going. You're gonna be late."

In the car ride to work, I again looked at my watch to see what new photo might appear but saw the same picture of Jack and my daughter. And again, when I got to my trailer. And again, during our lunch break, and when I got home, and before bed, and the next day, and the day after that. The face of the watch was no longer rotating the different photos chosen for it but instead held just this one. I checked the watch's app on my phone and reset it. But it was still stuck on Jack. It was stuck on Jack for a long time. How sweet, I thought, the universe keeping him close to me while abroad.

But my body told a different story each time I looked at the photo. I would feel physical unease: a sensation in my lower abdomen that would transmute with persistence all over. I directed all my senses toward the ache and then my mind, too. I asked what it was trying to tell me. What came back was a picture at first, painted in a thousand directives: an urgency to move, to travel somewhere far away, yet still familiar. To go somewhere distantly needed. I checked the watch again. Still Jack.

In that moment, my whole body spoke, and my mind heard what was being said. This stuck photo was a sign, for lack of a better word, and for lack of a better sign, this was also a word: *time*. Time, both literal and metaphorical, was trying to tell me something. In this moment, time was not just a clock on my wrist marking the hour, it was a countdown advancing toward something, as if these specific hours and these specific days meant more than just a passing but, perhaps, a disappearing.

I needed to go west. I needed to see Jack as soon as possible.

That evening, I emailed him and told him I wanted to come visit as soon as I could leave Canada. I wanted to come to San Francisco where he lived with his wife, the poet Agneta Falk, and I wanted to bring Marlow, too. Neither of us had seen Jack and Aggie for more than a year and a half because of the COVID-19 pandemic, and working abroad had furthered the absence of that time between us.

*Time.*

"Jack!" I emailed him that night. "Are you and Aggie in SF around the week of August 9? I might be coming to town with Marlow and just wanted to see if you'd be there."

"*Cara* Amber," he wrote back within the hour (*cara* meaning *dear* in Italian). "Yes, we're here. Looking forward to seeing you both. *Sempre*, Jack."

The body always knows first. It knows through sensation, or the absence of it, what happened before, what's happening now, what's to come. The mind comprehends what the body knows, eventually, and in that comprehension, the mind makes a swift decision about the information imparted and whether that information threatens the stability of the person inhabiting the body. The body might tell you that you have to run, for office or from a relationship. It might tell you to fight back, from a predator or the tears in your eyes. It tells us something's wrong: we are sick or someone else is. It tells us things before our mind can: we're in love, it's possible to heal whole parts of ourselves, we're hitting a creative threshold, or something is coming to an end.

Our mind weighs this information and often errs on the side of caution, not wanting to cause disruption even when this information might mean a breakthrough, a revolutionary idea, or a reclamation. The mind can be our strongest protector, the armor over our adventure, the sorcerer behind the spun tales of our mythology: what we need to tell ourselves to survive. Because, even though the body knows first, on its own, it's not always right in its reaction. It can tell us that we are not worthy of touch, that we are broken when we are not, that we should be afraid to act on what we feel. The body on its own can send mixed signals, second-guess itself, or put itself in a dangerous situation. (Think of all the times you've said, "I wasn't thinking" and you meant it.) Similarly, the mind on its own can be misleading, causing us to spiral down into irrationalities or stubbornly carb-load on what's safest: analysis and intellectualization. And somewhere amid the handoff between the body's knowing and the mind's grasp of it, somewhere before the swift decision but after the sensation, somewhere in the meet-cute between the two, there's a window worth listening in to. It can tell us when to move into action, or when to nest, when to say goodbye, when to go west. What you will hear is your intuition.

"In biological terms, these telepathic responses to the distress of family members and close friends make good sense," writes researcher of parapsychology Rupert Sheldrake in his book, *The Sense of Being Stared At*, in what he describes as the effects of intentions at a distance. "They are not mere curiosities of marginal significance but are often important for survival." Sheldrake believes that a response to telepathic intuition has been proven to save lives in some cases, or at the very least, helped to comfort those who are in distress, even if acting on that intuitive calling is nothing more than a simple phone call.

For women, the actualizing of our intuition can be life-changing, but it requires long-term practice in earnest. What we call a gut feeling, or a hunch, or a voice inside, can be the driving force behind every decision we make, or every decision we don't. It is a way for us to hear what is needed, or what isn't, what is stopping us, or what won't let us begin. It can be what keeps us up at night, what makes us pull over on the side of the road, what propels us into a new career, or awakens us to the realization of an abuse. It is a second, deeper tongue which demands we speak. "This is why women are knowing creatures," writes poet, psychoanalyst and trauma specialist Clarissa Pinkola Estés in her iconic 1992 book, *Women Who Run With the Wolves: Myths and Stories of The Wild Woman Archetype*. "They are made, in essence, of the skin of the sole, which feels everything." If women are made from the soles of life's feet, then intuition is the ground on which we walk; the culmination of our instincts and the utilized connection between our physical bodies and the influence of our minds.

It is a tying of the knot between what can be explained and what cannot, and if we give it the power it deserves by strengthening its foundation within us, it can change us, and the world.

But if we choose to ignore our intuition, the consequences can be many. We end up with a life unfulfilled, a story unwritten, a body not saved, an unhealthy relationship continued. "Some women don't want to be in the psychic desert," writes Estés. "They hate the frailty, the sparceness of it. They keep trying to crank a rusty jalopy and pump their own way down the road to a fantasized shining city of the psyche. They are disappointed, for the lush and the wild is not there." Intuition might be something we are born with, but it is not something we are raised to maintain. From a young age, we are taught to grind down that connection between our bodies and our minds until it's a dull noise deep in the background of our daily doing. We are taught to do away with any gut feelings which paint us as difficult, controlling, dramatic, or unfit, even if those gut feelings might lead us toward a personal or professional revelation or freedom.

The destruction of our intuitive lives in our youth is the first major act of misogyny a young girl will experience in a life defined by the normalization of such oppressions. As young girls, we are often punished for exploring and expressing our emotions and demonized for wanting them to matter. We are told that rational and intellectual thought are the only worthy forms of intelligence, and we are groomed to believe that our bodies hold no importance other than to be objectified. We are encouraged to stay small, quiet, and polite as we grow up and move through a world that has built itself on the comfort of that normality. We are told to fit into that world, not stand out from it. Charm that world, heed that world, follow that world—do not try to make it yours. We are asked to be good mothers, good teachers, good writers, good doctors, good listeners, but to draw the line of that listening to when it is our own.

Still, we hear. We cannot help hearing. The window calls to us, demanding what must be heard. And while the world has tried to separate us from it, we can never be severed from it, that which is our ancient guiding principle, intuition, fully realized.

After my job in Toronto finished, I moved my family back to New York and left soon after to take a vacation in Georgia in the late summer of 2021. I planned to visit Jack and Aggie a month after I got back, and I called to tell him.

"Sounds good, kiddo," he said on the phone, his strong voice vibrating through my ear. "We'll be here and can't wait to see you."

A few weeks later, I was sitting on my sister-in-law's stoop drinking a cup of coffee under the hot Georgia morning sun when a text came in from my friend of twenty-five years, poet Derrick Brown. Jack had died in his sleep.

I did not believe it, could not believe it at first. I quickly went on the *San Francisco Chronicle*'s website to see, hoping it was some horrible mistake on Derrick's part. But it was true. It was true. I let out a fractured scream as my arms threw my phone onto the lawn in front of me. They stayed outstretched after it hit the grass, then reached out farther, up toward the sun as I came up onto my knees, grabbing at the sky in disbelief, trying to pull Jack back to me, to will his body home from its eternity. They say to never stare into the sun, that you can go blind, but that morning my eyes could not leave the confrontation of its horrible brightness, could not make sense of it as a symbol for future days in which Jack no longer existed. I stared into it, violent with grief, and could make out with watery eyes the edges of my fingers pulling at its fire. I would never see him again, except in pictures. I would never hear his bold growl of a voice on the phone, or receive his handwritten letters in the mail, or share a vodka with him at Specs' Bar, or walk with him down Columbus Avenue in San Francisco. He would never read my poems again, and I would never send them to him.

And there in the blazing light was the watch on my arm. And Jack's picture, pressed against an unrelenting sky. As I wept, I removed it from my wrist and held it to my lips, its face between my teeth, as if to swallow it whole, to make the image come back to life, to go back in time and get to him sooner.

*Time.*

Jack's time was running out, and then it was gone. Just like that. And it was my body and then my mind—my intuition—that had tried to prepare me for this moment by giving meaning and purpose to what was nothing more than a digital malfunction of hardware on my wrist. Time itself had not halted, but Jack's time *was* ceased, and the meaning of time, for me, had been altered by this symbolism— by this foreshadowing. Jack's face stuck in perpetuity on an

interface mere months before his death was probably just a
coincidence, but it was mine to intuit real meaning from.
And I did just that. Acting on my intuition, however late,
may not have resulted in getting to say goodbye to him, but
it got me closer than if I had ignored it. There would have
been no email exchanges, no last phone call, no intention
expressed in which I could hold on to for the rest of my life
as proof that at least *I tried*. Listening to my gut played an
integral part in some form of goodbye, which was not nothing. And it showed me that the window inside, the space
where the body knows and the mind receives, is worth listening in to, worth being guided by, and worth investing in.

Each of us has access to that window which unlocks our
intuitive process, and for each of us, there is a road map
that points to exactly how we can harness it, each and
every time. This book aims to acknowledge and pinpoint
that process: to excavate a clear and concise path toward
embracing and activating your own intuitive intelligence,
and to be able to use it at will. Within these pages, you
will read from powerful women across industries: doctors,
actresses, biologists, politicians, writers, composers, poets,
comedians, and even my own mother, all of whom have
spent their lives cultivating a profound relationship with
an intuition which has been used to actualize their greatest potentials, and even change the world.

The activation of intuition presents differently in every
woman, and this book intends to teach each and every
one of us how to access our own, uniquely and individually. For some women, this feeling may present first in the

body: an agitation, a doubt, an unquenchable urgency. It may be unexplainable, what you can't quite put a finger on, though your spirit demands you must. It is what compels you, even when you may not want to. "Go back to that one red flower and walk straight ahead for that last hard mile," writes Estés. "Go up and knock on the old weathered door. Climb up to the cave. Crawl through the window of the dream. Sift the desert and see what you find. It is the only work we *have* to do." Follow the voice inside that compels you to that sealed windowsill, when a defining moment of your life calls for deep introspection, when you are pushed to change, to fight, to leave, to stay, or to speak.

It is both a window you must learn to look and listen out from, and a window of time in which you have to do it. *Time.*

Follow your arms, outstretched, to find the answer and the bravery to bring it to fruition. See your fingers reaching, pushing up, until that window is no longer closed. Trust that gravitation: a pulling which makes you and only you its orbit. Trust yourself; trust your process; trust your map. See the stories from this collection—their triumphs, reckonings, and revelations—as a compass which can show you a direction—a way to begin.

So begin. Follow your map. Find your window. Take in what your body can hear and your mind can achieve when you're wide open, listening in the dark.

# Over the Rainbow

By Dr. Mindy Nettifee
*Depth Psychology Researcher and Poet*

In my early thirties, my boyfriend of nine years and I decided to get married. There was no proposal, no ring, just a series of casual-then-increasingly-not-casual conversations in which we generally agreed it was time to move forward. Marriage seemed like a logical next step. My sudden openness to this came as a surprise to me. I had previously been sure that marriage, in general, was not something I wanted to be a part of. While I was a cisgender woman partnered with a cisgender man and monogamously so, I identified as bisexual and queer. At the time, gay marriage was still illegal in the state of California, where we lived, and it didn't feel right taking part in something others couldn't. The institution of marriage itself seemed unrepentantly rotten, unhealed at its patriarchal core.

Even setting those reservations aside, however, I felt split. One part of me, the part I most identified with, truly loved this man, this kind, moody guitarist I had mooned over all through my twenties. We had some serious issues: he had cheated on me, he tended to shut down emotionally whenever conflict arose, and he had a lot of growing up to do. But I had a lot of growing up to do, too. I wasn't perfect, and I didn't need him to be perfect either. We had come through so much together, and I could not imagine my life without him. This part of me wondered whether a ceremony formalizing our commitment to each other might actually be what was missing: a catalyst for growth.

Another part of me, a shadowy, shy part, saw things differently, and would sometimes rise to the surface dramatically. I would walk into the living room and see this grown man playing video games, and it was like a fog lifting. I would suddenly know with total, sobering clarity that while I loved this person, I did not fully trust him. I didn't feel safe with him or understood by him, and I did not want to have a family or a future with him. Not only should I not marry him, I should leave; I should stop compromising. It was not about finding someone perfect, but it *was* about finding someone perfect for me. He wasn't.

When I consulted these conflicting parts in turn, both felt right, both felt instinctual. Which one was the voice of my intuition, my deep inner knowing, and which one was the voice of my fear? I had no idea and no way of finding out. So I erred on the side of preserving the relationship. To quell some of my reservations, we decided not to get an official marriage license; we would have what everyone could have, a commitment ceremony. As the date of our planned ceremony approached, the struggle between these parts of myself amplified. I overrode my hesitancy in the way many nervous brides do—with champagne. We had a lovely, joyous, irreverent wedding in the hills of Ojai with all our family and friends. And then I waited for all my parts to settle, for the inner voices to relax, for my fears to subside.

They didn't. My sense that I had made a terrible mistake got steadily worse. I kept busy. I poured myself into work. I exercised diligently to manage my anxiety. When that wasn't enough, I started smoking cigarettes here and there, did a little day drinking. I made increasingly elaborate meals, his favorite meals. I doubled my efforts in the bedroom. I gratitude-journaled like never before. I was a working artist at the time, a performance poet, and something told me to begin planning a tour and pour all my free time and attention into it.

On the day before I was set to leave on this month-long tour that would take me up and down the West Coast, then to Arizona, then to Hawaii, I got a brief email from my partner's mother. It was about three months past our wedding now, and she wanted to know what county we had filed our marriage license in, to put in some sort of official family record. She said she had asked her son already, and he had claimed not to remember and told her to ask me about it. I was instantly furious. *Why had he lied to his mother?* Why didn't she call him out on this obvious lie? Like, why wouldn't he remember where we had filed our marriage license, if indeed we had filed one? Why had he put me in a position to either further the lie about the marriage license or tell his mother that he had lied to her?

The voice, the shadow voice, surged. I felt something like a foreshock before an earthquake.

I knew a big, life-altering fight was coming, but I didn't want to have it and then leave town. So I pressed pause. I told myself the fight could wait. I would not confront my partner about the email until I returned from this tour. In the meantime, I would get some space to process, and maybe my anger would burn through its fuel a bit. Smart. Logical. I went back to my to-do list. I think I started packing a suitcase with merch. And then this really small thing happened.

My partner had given me a solar-powered rainbow maker as a gift. It hung from the living room window, and when the sun was shining at the right angle, its colorful gears would turn, which would then turn attached prisms that would cast little rainbows all around the room. It was a gift I had specifically asked for, and I loved it. I loved rainbows! As I was packing for the tour, the sun was streaming through the window, and the rainbows were dancing. All of a sudden, I heard this small sound, like a snap, and looked up to see the rainbows had stopped moving. I went to investigate what had happened, and there it was, broken; one of its gears, the little pink one, had just snapped. I immediately felt some foreboding. It meant something, but I didn't know what exactly.

The next morning, I kissed my husband and left for the tour, haunted by his mother's email and the broken pink gear. I was touring with two other poets, one I knew very well and loved and one I hardly knew at all but instantly liked. We called ourselves The Whirlwind Company. We started down in San Diego and performed poetry each night in a new city. Each day we drove for hours, talking and singing in the car with the windows rolled down. It was fall, and as we headed north, the weather began to turn, the leaves aflame with reds and oranges and golds. It was mostly a perfect escape. But in quiet moments my troubles lingered; wherever you go, there you are. I would ruminate on my situation, my potentially-marrying-the-wrong-person situation, and feel sick to my stomach. But for the first time, the shy, shadowy voice began to dominate. For the first time perhaps, I allowed myself to imagine leaving, not just for a tour but leaving the relationship. It was such a painful thought, I could only stay with it a minute at a time. But each day, I could stay with it a little longer.

There was also something new and wild and alive in me, something awake that felt unaffected by my troubles. Maybe it was just the medicine of distance or the effect of breaking away from familiar routines. I had an energy I hadn't felt in a long time. When we crossed the border from California into Oregon, it was like I was leaving a state of being behind. I felt looser, freer. This awakeness was now even more awake. That's when I saw it—one of the largest rainbows I had ever seen in my life, love-beaming across the entire highway like the smile of some ecstatic god. It was fat and bright and achingly beautiful. We all agreed it was a sign, a blessing that our time in Oregon would be great, and we cheered as we drove under it.

A few miles down the highway, another rainbow, this one wider and brighter, appeared. I squealed and let out a cry. A few more miles and yet another rainbow appeared, this time a double, like a chord and its harmonic, like a power ballad of color. My heart was bursting, and I could no longer drive. I pulled off the road so one of my tour mates could take the wheel, and I could melt down safely on the passenger side. We saw close to forty rainbows that day, driving the Interstate 5 corridor through the center of Oregon. I was so drunk on rainbows and beauty I could no longer speak. I thought of that little rainbow maker and its snapped gear. The metaphor was clear: my current relationship had a broken gear. Even if I could fix it, there was something relatively small and manufactured about its joys, I could see that now. If I was willing to be brave and leave the life I knew behind, following the call of this other voice, this wild knowing, something bigger, something more beautiful, something much more real awaited me.

Nothing happened immediately. I had to finish my tour despite my deepening realization that I needed to change course. Also, my newfound intuitive clarity didn't make the changes ahead less excruciating. Imagining hurting this person I loved, imagining letting everyone down was terrifying. And even after I returned home from tour, I still couldn't act. I had all these other instincts to contend with—instincts to stay safe, to stay loyal, to avoid pain, to be sweet and nice and prioritize the needs and feelings of others. Every time I felt the courage to speak, it felt like the gas and the brake were being hit at the same time. My throat would close up. I would start to leave my body a little. Then I would back off, breathe, and wait another day.

I finally went to see someone I trusted—an acupuncturist who always seemed to know very detailed, very personal things about me just by feeling my pulse. Her sense of what was going on with me was always uncannily accurate. It felt like a final intervention to all my inaction. I believed that if I was actually going crazy and doing something self-destructive, she would know; she would check my vitals and frown and give it to me straight. Instead, when she felt my pulse that day, she reported that for the first time ever, everything seemed completely in balance. I went home that day and had the first of several devastating conversations that would completely undo my life.

I was unprepared for how difficult it would be intentionally hurting someone I loved and how scary it would be to go out into the world alone, without a partner, without a home, having alienated my friends and family. In spite of my strong sense that I was doing the right thing, I still felt a lot of shame. All my social and cultural conditioning was still a part of me. That epic host of rainbows had liberated me from playing it safe and small, but they couldn't completely scrub my psyche of its old survival strategies of submissive appeasement. I felt heavy with selfishness. I was carrying the disappointment and disapproval of others, some of it real, some of it imagined. I was also grieving but felt undeserving of sympathy or compassion. I pushed through because I had to. My intuition told me I must, even though there would be very little evidence, for years, that everything was going to be okay.

I can say now, unequivocally, that following that shadowy, intuitive voice over a decade ago radically changed my life for the better. Since then, I have properly and wholeheartedly committed to an incredible life partner and devoted myself to study and work in the fields of somatics and depth psychology, helping other people find and fix their own broken gears. I was not aware of the extent to which I was not being true to myself until I started listening to that voice and following it, and even then, it was a slow unveiling.

In the West, we have a way of talking about this kind of profound split from the self in terms of the conscious and the unconscious. We use light as a metaphor for awareness and the conscious mind, tying it to our embodied experience of vision. An idea can be *illuminating* or *brilliant*. When we understand something, we say, "I *see*." Similarly, we use darkness as a metaphor for the unconscious. When we refer to work with the unconscious, we might call it *shadow* work. This darkness is only in reference to our lack of awareness, not its ultimate value. We can repress awareness of our *dark side*, sure: the parts of us that we judge as ugly or deviant, that aren't *the real us*, our meanness and jealousy and arrogance. But we can also repress awareness of our best inner resources, our power and talent and confidence. If you live in a family or culture where you aren't allowed to shine, you might repress all that shininess to survive.

Unconscious complexes and defenses are extremely powerful forces and upset our notions of agency. Depth psychologist Donald Kalsched calls our unconscious defenses our "self-care system," in wise acknowledgment that their ultimate purpose is self-protection, and we should speak about them respectfully, as defending ourselves against our defenses won't get us anywhere. Once these defenses form in response to frightening or painful experiences, they are capable of driving our behavior beneath the level of our conscious awareness in both creative and destructive ways. They can cut off from conscious awareness any memories or feelings or inner conflicts that are too overwhelming or threatening. They can also drive us back toward wholeness. What I experienced in my early thirties was an eruption from my unconscious, the surfacing of a part of me that my defenses were keeping at bay because it threatened the safety of the status quo.

In the months before my doomed wedding ceremony, I had published a collection of poems called *Rise of the Trust Fall*. Yeah... Poems bore eerily familiar titles like "In Our Bedroom, Before the War," "Don't Pretend You Don't Know What to Do," and "To the Best Thing That Ever Happened to Me," the latter of which was about a woman who escapes the man who wants to marry her and ends up stuck in a snowdrift(!). My intuitive knowing that my relationship was ending was still hidden from me, buried in the unconscious. While I wrote these poems, I was not aware that they reflected my own reality. I thought they were *just* creations. That's how it works: if something is unconscious, it doesn't matter if you're staring right at it, you won't see it. Or you might see it for a fleeting moment, and then—blink—it's gone. You've forgotten it.

My reckoning with my own experience of the unconscious–conscious divide led me to want to learn more about human psychology, though that desire, too, arrived like an irrational impulse. I was a poet by profession, and if I wanted to do some graduate study, the logical choice would have been to pursue an MFA in creative writing. But every time I considered that seriously, my whole being would resist. Luckily, I had found a question that served as a kind of key for accessing my intuition, that part of me untouched by social conditioning: *What would I do if I didn't have to explain it to anybody?*

This question led me to the next intuitive move: pursuing a doctorate in depth psychology with a specialization in somatics. I wanted to know more about the mysteries of neurobiology and the mind–body spectrum. My intuition guided me throughout my studies. While its impulses almost always initially seemed irrational and in direct contradiction to what I thought I knew, they always led me in the direction of greater creativity, growth, understanding, and wholeness. I learned to trust them, or rather, I learned how to negotiate with the parts of me that did not trust them.

Here's how I've come to understand it. There is a radical physical intelligence in me, a bodily wisdom. When I am connected to myself in this way, I can clearly sense what's not right for me, what doesn't feel safe or good, and where I feel a boundary or a *no*. I can also feel what is right for me, what's a *yes*, what might be beneficial to my well-being and my growth. It is limited to the present moment—I cannot accurately sense something far in the future—and it's limited to addressing questions that can be answered with *yes/no/wait*. What I call my intuition is entangled with my physical intelligence. It can signal me through sensations felt in my body: a physical urge to contract or pull away, a physical urge to go toward, a little squeeze of affirmation in my inner ear, a shiver up my spine. It can also signal me through my imagination or my dreams, sending me images or ideas that directly transmit their meaning.

When the pink gear snapped, that was what depth psychologists call a synchronicity—a moment when an inner event and an outer event meet—and it amplified the emerging voice of my intuition so it could finally break through my defenses and be fully felt and heard. It's not that all pink gears mean something. Rather, I was a poet. Metaphor was a strong channel of perception for me in a way that, at the time, body sensations were not. So the pink gear of a rainbow maker snapping followed by an encounter with a host of real rainbows had the effect of getting through to me; it was a sign of what I already, deep down, knew to be true for me.

The more I learned about the psyche and the body and its complex personal and collective layers, the more I came to respect my struggle to distinguish intuitive knowing from conditioning or fear. My ability to connect with myself in this way had been compromised by a great deal of trauma and abuse in my early life—sexual abuse, poverty, and struggling caregivers, just to name a few. Defending myself in any of these cases by fighting or fleeing was not possible. The strategies my unconscious self-care system employed to survive were what was available to me as a child: sweetness and easiness, submission to and appeasement of those in power, and dissociation into my imagination. While they allowed me to survive, they shaped me fundamentally. I came into adulthood with almost no sense of what my own needs were, how to sense a boundary, or how to defend a boundary when it was challenged rather than overriding it to avoid conflict with others. The part of me that wanted to stay in that relationship, to stay safe, that couldn't ever imagine leaving or hurting someone else, even if my needs weren't being met, that was all that old survival physiology.

It took me years of therapy and somatic learning to heal enough and develop enough to feel like I could reliably discern my intuition from the fear of past trauma and conditioning—especially because my intuition is regularly urging me in the direction of uncomfortable or frightening growth edges. But neuroplasticity is real; healing and changing even very deep patterns is possible. I was so moved by what I learned in my own healing process, by everything I discovered about the body and intuition, I began training as a somatic trauma therapist in addition to completing my doctoral studies. My dissertation research focused on the impact of trauma on the voice and expression—our ability to know what's true for ourselves and be honest. I now get to accompany people through their own journey of healing and reconnection with their own intuition and power and voice.

What continues to fascinate me is how intuition connects us to something larger than us and can guide us beyond the limits of our current conscious knowing. While I was following one intuitive impulse at a time, having no idea where it would lead, I experienced the seeming magic, over and over, of intuitive timing. The Greeks called it *kairos* time, meaning *the opportune moment*. It's very different from linear *chronos* time that gives us clocks and calendars and five-year plans. *Kairos* is a nonlinear, spiraling, tidal kind of time. *Chronos* helps us follow through on a conscious agenda; *kairos* helps us move beyond that agenda. For example, I had no idea when I set out to study depth psychology and somatics that I would end up studying trauma and the voice, but I happened to be in the middle of my dissertation research on this subject when Tarana Burke's #MeToo movement surged. Where just weeks before there had been little public discourse about post-traumatic silence and what it takes to overcome it, now it was everywhere. It was as if I had timed it intentionally, but I could not have.

Our personal and collective trauma is so great, its roots so deep. We have a lot of healing and evolving to do as a species if we have any hope of surviving ourselves. The time of consequences and unraveling is already here. The gear has snapped. We won't get where we need to go with what we already know, by approaching *knowing* itself in the same ways. I am speaking of us Westerners, living in a culture that values the objective, rational mind (the rational white male European mind) above the feeling, sensing body. As we open up to intuition, as we develop and refine our sensitivity and attunement to our own bodies and the bodies of others, we tap the intelligence of the natural world, and something bigger and wilder than just ourselves: we tap the wisdom of the whole. It might feel like we are following rainbows, and we are.

# Untwisting My Intuition

By Jessica Valenti
*Writer*

For most of my life, I have not been able to trust my gut. That inner voice meant to protect me has been twisted and warped by a lifetime of negative messages reinforcing what I grew up believing to be true: that I don't know what I'm talking about, or that what's happening to me, what I'm feeling, is just something I'm imagining. For years, my intuition was silenced by the world around me, which gave it no space to grow or define itself. It felt like the whisper of lies in my ear, rather than something that might lead me to safety.

There was a voice in my head that told me I was a terrible mother for not producing enough breast milk for my premature daughter, and a sinking gut feeling that said I was overreacting whenever a boyfriend treated me poorly or a married male friend started making advances. *You're being dramatic*, it whispered. *It's not that bad.*

My relationship to that voice inside hadn't always been

like this, and I can remember what the beginnings of a healthy, glowing intuition felt like when I was younger. I remember a kind of knowing I possessed as a young girl—the kind of intuition that just knew the reason the boys in second grade didn't want me on their baseball team during gym wasn't because I wasn't good—I *knew* I was—it was because they were wrong.

But as I grew older, I began to learn how to do what all the other young women were also being taught to do. We were being shown that our emotions were too loud, our instincts too wrong, and we'd better learn how to quiet them. As I grew up, what I knew to be true started to turn into what I knew I should question or be ashamed of.

As a child, I remember watching my father scream at my mother, throwing a chair at her across the dining room. I know I hated him in that moment, understanding that what he was doing was bad. But the more I saw her shrink into herself, walking on eggshells around him, the more my gut said *Your mother is weak, she sets him off, don't be like her—don't show how you feel and what you know.* My father got to act with impunity and get whatever he wanted, and I was modeled how to get quiet and stay there.

It was self-preservation, to be sure: better to identify with the person who seems stronger so you're not the person getting yelled at. But as my intuition continued to wither, unsure what was real and what wasn't, it failed in even the most basic ways to keep me safe.

When I was twelve and a man started to masturbate on a subway platform in front of me while I waited for the train to take me to school, I convinced myself that I must be mistaken. That I couldn't trust my own eyes. *You don't need to run from this man on the subway, just stand there and take it. Do nothing. That is what's safest.*

My intuition and what I knew to be right or wrong were being chipped away every day, and as I grew into my teenage years, I often thought my gut reaction and my oppression were one and the same. When I was eighteen and walking down the sidewalk on my way to the first day of an internship, a man in a car pulled over and asked for directions. My gut was silent, as it had learned how to become. It didn't tell me anything was amiss or that I should be mindful of talking to strange men on empty streets so early in the morning that it was still dark out. Instead, I cheerily stepped off the curb to help him—close enough to his car that he was able to grab my arm and try to pull me in through his window. It wasn't until I was halfway into his car, his breath hot on my cheek, that I realized his penis was out.

I don't know how I was able to free myself. I don't have any memory of it. But I know that I ran toward home and knocked on the door of my aunt's house who shared a yard with us. She gave me a shot of some kind of alcohol, I don't know what, to calm my nerves and told me, unequivocally, how stupid I was to step off that damned curb. It wasn't said cruelly; she was right and trying to help, and these are the lessons passed down between generations of women to try and protect us. In her own way, she wasn't just trying to knock some sense into me but rattle my gut reaction awake so it could do its damn job. After all, I had lived in Queens my whole life. I should have known better.

By this point in my life, my inner voice was almost completely trained not to hold my best interests at heart but to align with those of men and what they wanted from me. How could it not? It had been scolded by teachers who rolled their eyes when I asked questions, family who told me not to be so loud and emotional, and commercials and TV shows that told me that the best version of myself was always going to be the pretty, polite, naive one. Year by year, my ability to be able to tell what was right and what was wrong—who was safe and who was not—became broken. And I was broken along with it.

Without the strength of an inner compass I could trust to guide me, I made all the wrong turns, often telling myself they were the right ones, because that's what I believed to be true. I chose the wrong men, the wrong friends, the wrong classes and jobs. If I couldn't trust myself, I'd trust everyone else, even if most people weren't worthy of it.

As I became a young woman, I started to feel betrayed by my own intuition—or what I thought my intuition was. I wasn't sure whose interests it was serving. I felt abandoned by myself almost entirely, my relationship to my intuitive process irrevocably distorted.

It was only when I started asking why I couldn't trust myself—questioning how and when it happened—that I was able to piece together an answer that helped move me forward.

I stumbled into women's studies classes and read feminists that put language to all of the unspeakable things I had in my head—women like bell hooks and magazines like *Bitch*. I started to see my own silencing reflected in their stories of survival, and as I read about all the ways in which they had learned to listen and trust themselves, I started to feel lighter.

It wasn't me, I realized, that was the problem. I was damaged, to be sure, but not innately. I had been taught, over and over again, to be this way—to distrust my guts—because even though I was the casualty, it still benefited the world around me. The more unsure I was, the more I couldn't trust myself—the better for a country that depended on that uncertainty and self-consciousness to thrive. I would buy more, question less.

I started to forgive myself for all the things that broken inner voice had said to me in my worst moments and began to recognize it as a symptom of its own oppressive conditioning. I called them what they were: lies to keep me sated. I realized that my intuition wasn't dead—that it was just hidden. After all, finally learning how to listen to it was what had led me to question all of this in the first place.

That doesn't mean I was able to trust myself overnight, or that I was able to tell the true from the untrue all at once. My strategy, instead, became to do the opposite of what my patriarchy-shaped gut told me to do.

When I met my husband, I had to actively work against that oppressive inner voice born so long ago when I was younger, just to be able to receive his affection and love. I realized that the only way I was going to be happy was to not give in to that old way of talking to myself but, instead, to do the exact opposite and fight to hear that voice inside that believed in me.

And it worked. I got the life I wanted by actively interrogating and questioning the part of me that wanted to tear me down and see me fail. Why did I want to get blackout drunk? How was it serving me? Why did I fuck up good friendships and embrace the bad ones? What if I just…didn't?

I started to make good decisions, even when that bad voice inside was telling me not to. I let myself be scared and self-conscious when I decided to start writing professionally. I allowed for discomfort when I broke off habits and relationships. I ignored the remnants of my fragmented inner voice and did the things that felt all wrong.

Of course, what was really happening wasn't that I was rejecting my true inner voice: I was just learning how to use it again, stretching and working it like an atrophied muscle that needed daily exercises to become strong again. My real intuition was peeking through the rubble, letting me know that it had always been there. I just wasn't ready to find it yet.

To this day, a clear and easy line to my intuition is still a struggle, but I believe this is all part of the process. My gut is a shifting, evolving thing which can't help but be influenced by the patriarchal world, and which has undergone decades worth of gaslighting and trauma. There is still a voice inside that overshadows the better parts of me. It's the voice that still says I'm not good enough for my husband, or that despite years of feminist work that I'm a fraud. *Come on, you know I'm right. Just this once.*

But its begging is a warning sign I now pay attention to. Instead of giving in, I return to the signals of my body: my toes that grab sand, my fingers that type, my chest that my daughter loves to lay her head on. Most of the time, it works.

I've built a life protected with people who love me, people I can trust; they are the safety net when I can't fully rely on myself to know what the right answer is. I can ask those loving and loved people what they think is actually best for me, and together, we will find the answer. They've become extensions of my intuition, safeguards that I've put in place to make sure I remember who I really am and what I really want.

And so today, I try to trust my intuition—and when I can't, I trust my community.

# The Science of Intuition and Deep Connection with Nature

By Dr. Nicole Apelian
*Survivalist and Anthropologist*

*The intuitive mind is a sacred gift and the rational mind is a faithful servant. We have created a society that honors the servant and has forgotten the gift.*

**—Albert Einstein**

As the helicopter descended into the remote site on Vancouver Island, I was overcome with a feeling of thrill and excitement. It dropped me off in the wilderness, away from civilization, with no way to contact anyone except for an emergency-only satellite phone. I watched as the aircraft took off into the sky, and as the silence enveloped me I thought to myself, *Alone... Alone at last.*

I was out in the forests of Canada participating in a reality television series for the History Channel called *Alone*, a show where participants must survive in isolation out in the wild, completely on their own, with a very limited amount of survival equipment. We had to learn how to film ourselves, having trained pre-show on the use of six different cameras, and had to fend for ourselves in a challenging landscape with tough weather. My particular location in northwest Vancouver Island gets ten-plus feet of rain per year, and most of that rain took place in the fall and winter seasons while I was there. The above description may sound daunting, but for me it was a two-month-long journey filled with joy. It was a time of living in the now, where my daily to-do list was simple: fire, shelter, water, and food. My primal intuitive brain was open, forgotten neurons were reawakened, and I could hear and feel every ripple of the environment surrounding me.

The first few weeks out in the wilderness were busy ones. I used skills I've studied all my life as a survivalist, biologist, and anthropologist to set up my new life there in the woods, for however long the journey would last for me. My skills come naturally to me: setting up shelter, a place for a fire, trapping, and hunting. There's no stress, no worry. My body became an efficient machine as my wiry frame sawed, cut, and built. Every day there was much to do: build my new home, gather firewood, forage and hunt for food, set traps to work for me while I slept. Fire came easily. Heading into this adventure, fire and hypothermia were my main worries out in these wet, cold woods. For a month prior I'd been soaking cedar bark in a tub of water overnight. Every morning I'd take out the sopping wet bark and work it until I had a dry tinder bundle that I could light with a spark from my ferro rod, a human-made metal stick that is used to create fire, as matches and lighters are not allowed on the show. My daily practice paid off.

While on the show, I lived alone in a thick shelter that

I built with my own two hands, made out of the forest's debris, sleeping on a raised log bed with a thick mattress of cedar and hemlock boughs cut using my large survival knife. I brought in hot rocks from my fire at night to make my primitive shelter toasty warm in just a few minutes. I saw many predators (wolves, cougars, and bears) and heard the songs of the native birds in the area. I had built in me a deep sensory awareness—an intuition—about the language of the birds and that of the predators around me from living in the bushveld along the Okavango Delta in northern Botswana, where I once was an African lion researcher in the 1990s. Because of this experience, I forged a powerful alliance with my most primitive intuitiveness, which allowed me to live side by side with the creatures there. I was careful with the cougars, respectful of the bears, and a student of the wolves around me.

I love being in the woods. I am not bored, and I feel my healthiest when I'm outdoors, eating the wild foods from the earth and listening to the sounds of nature alone everywhere around me.

A family of bears lived close by my shelter, and we had an agreement to leave each other be, which I intuited from being in community with them. The moment of my arrival, I saw their tracks and knew there was a mom with cubs who lived there. I stated, "I'm here in peace. Your cubs are safe," so that she would know my intentions were good. One day, I saw the black bear family. They appeared from the south side of the bay, and the mom came out first, the cubs following her as they broke out of a thick alder-salmonberry patch. As she came onto the floodplain the young 'uns started playing and tumbling. It was a joy to watch. I was not in fear, and I sensed they were not threatened by me. The mother peered into the river, probably looking for the same thing I was: salmon. We were both successful, day in and out, to the point where once *Alone* premiered on TV, I became known as the Salmon Slayer for my pan full of salmon steaks. I loved to watch the mama and her cubs play on the beach nearby, and when I needed to go up their side of the river, I would make sure to let them know out loud: "Human coming...bup bup bup bup bup!" I would say this so as not to surprise the mom. I would often go up their river into the deep thick brush to scavenge for salmon innards from their meals, which I would use to bait my hooks, catching dogfish and kelp bass for dinner.

Bears usually check out camps as they're curious creatures. But these bears never ventured close to my shelter (though a lone cougar did once). I put my shelter far enough away from any freshwater source that they had no reason to visit other than curiosity. Perhaps their curiosity had been satisfied seeing me on the beach, hearing my initial call of peace, and smelling my scent on the gill net that I used to catch fish.

Intuition is not just something I use to survive, it is something I use to communicate with the wildlife living alongside me.

One time, after I moved my gill net up into the intertidal zone so harbor seals would stop stealing my salmon, I saw the four-hundred-pound papa bear emerge on the beach, thirty yards to my east. He disappeared briefly before re-emerging, walking west along the beach until he stopped at my net and sniffed my fresh human scent on the posts I'd just repounded into the hard, pebbled sand. In an instant, he turned and lumbered straight toward me. I saw him so clearly, every ripple of his muscles as he walked, the wetness of his paws, his eyes fixed both ahead and directly on me. I was not afraid, because I speak his language: we share the same voice inside that tells us of each other's intentions. Just as I started to doubt myself, he veered off to the right and sank back into the woods, forming a wide berth around my shelter.

After this introduction, the male bear and I would often forage together on the beach, side by side. We gave each other our space but were fully aware that we were there together, eating the same foods. He was good company, much to the surprise of the production crew who came by boat to swap out a camera I'd dropped in the water (the wind had knocked my tripod over into the sea). I was raising my gill net when they arrived, having caught a salmon that day, and my bear friend took off as they hit shore.

"Did you know there was a bear *right there*?" said one of the crew members with concern. "It was really close to you."

I smiled and said I did. *Alone... Alone at last.*

Clear communication is intuition at its highest form. Animals don't override their intuition because they can't afford to: they have to use it constantly to survive. Think of the way your dog knows you are coming home before you even turn onto the street. However, we as humans have forgotten the daily practice of this communication, which requires us to use both what we've intellectually learned and what we intuitively know at the same time. We have forgotten because we lack the daily primal connection that these animals must have and use. We have modern visual, auditory, and physical distractions, and almost constant chatter in our brains: cell phones, social media, computers, and so much more. The chaos and perpetual presence of these distracters don't allow us to hear in the many ways that the natural world does. To reconnect to our primal selves and to the intuition that must guide us through the chaos, we have to follow the Buddhist mantra: *Chop wood, carry water: master your connection to your intuitive life and the simple necessities of survival, and all the miracles around you will be revealed.*

After the thirty-day mark of being alone, time slowed down. My biggest chores and goals were completed. My home, sheltered by a two-hundred-foot grandmother spruce, was warm and dry, complete with a handmade door, a moss-chinked cabin front, and an awning extension, which served as a place outside to shelter away from the constant driving rain. My thick, comfy bough bed sported a headboard, footboard, and side rails, enveloping me in evergreen scent. I had enough firewood and kindling cut and stacked to last a month. The rain was so plentiful that my water cache was always full. Daily chores still included firewood-gathering and adding debris to both my bed and shelter for increased insulation as the temperature dropped and winter began to set in. My daily rhythm was connected to the natural world. Food-gathering from the ocean was tied to the tides, so I was tied to the tides. Forgotten natural rhythms of the moon and sun governed my days. Gathering food took energy, but food was abundant there. I counted twenty-six species of food that I ingested, including fire-roasted banana slugs, fresh chanterelle mushrooms, silverweed roots, bullwhip kelp, limpets, and, of course, hand-caught salmon. Water, shelter, fire, food.

Being alone in the woods is raw and back to the basics for survival. It is physiologically and psychologically cleansing. There is a forced simplicity that takes place, a refocusing on only the bare essentials. Life is only occurring in the present moment. Free time is abundant. I made baskets and carved tools. I'd sit at my southeast-facing spot multiple times a day, a place with a beautiful view where I could commune with the natural world without thought, except when the storms were too strong to be outside safely. Those days, I would hole up in my cozy shelter, inside my mind, listening to large trees and branches crash down, competing with the waves for the loudest sound. I found I liked my company and was not bored at all. All my physical needs were met, and I was at one with my environment, happy, content.

Suddenly, on day fifty-seven of my time out in the wilderness, another voice called to me. It was not my own nor that of the bears nor other wildlife there. It was my twelve-year-old son. My gut told me I needed to go to him. I picked up the emergency phone and told the producers I was done, it was time to leave. Just like that, I knew it was time to go—to leave this remote home and return to my former one.

A few hours later I was on a boat headed back to Port Hardy, British Columbia, and was soon surrounded by four walls and my child. My son needed my love and my physical presence by his side. It had been the right choice, and I'd do it again in a heartbeat.

When you are connected to your intuition and your quieted mind is open to what can be received, you can hear these types of calls. The call home from my son was as clear as if he had picked up the phone and rung me himself. It was evident that he needed his mom, and he needed her *now*. And I was right. I thought of my kids a lot while I was out there in the woods alone, but I always knew that they were in good hands. I also knew that they would want me to do well, so I told myself that missing them would not be reason enough to go home. I stayed strong in that. However, intuiting a call from my son—one that I definitely knew was coming directly from him and not just my longing to see him again—was a different story.

To understand our intuition, we must first understand the literal science and mechanism of it: the enteric gut-brain connection. While the white matter in our brain transmits information, gray matter collects and modifies that information. Only twenty percent of the brain's gray matter is utilized for our rational mind, while a whopping eighty percent is dedicated to the unconscious mind. Intuition bridges the gap between the conscious and unconscious parts of our mind.[1] The gut feeling we have is a somatic manifestation—i.e., a physical response—of what our enteric gut-brain is trying to tell us.[2]

---

1    Reference: Cholle, Francis P., *The Intuitive Compass: Why the Best Decisions Balance Reason and Instinct* (San Francisco, CA: Jossey-Bass, 2011).

2    Reference: LeBoon, Richard, "Rethinking Intuition: Using the Framework of an Integrative-Brain Assessment for Optimal Decision-Making" (2018). Master of Philosophy in Organizational Dynamics Theses. 13.

### What is our gut-brain and how does it work?

We have three brains in our body: the heart-brain, the head-brain, and the gut-brain. Each has its own complex systems of neural networks. The heart-brain (or intrinsic cardiac nervous system) is the smallest, containing about forty thousand cardiac neurons. The head-brain is the largest, with about eighty-six billion neurons. The gut-brain, or enteric nervous system (ENS), is housed inside the walls of our digestive tract and is made up of two thin layers of more than a hundred million nerve cells that line our gastrointestinal tract from our esophagus to our rectum.[3]

While the gut-brain's chief function is to keep digestion moving properly and to maximize nutrient absorption, the ENS (gut-brain) can do something most of our neural networks can't: it can function independently. Our gut-brain can act autonomously and doesn't need to rely on signals from the central nervous system the way our other brains do. The autonomous ability has earned it the nickname the *second brain*. Additionally, in evolutionary terms, it is most likely much older and may be regarded as the body's first brain.[4]

Our gut sends over four hundred times more messages *from* the gut microbiomes to the brain in our head than from the brain back down to the gut.[5] Your gut is alert-

3   https://www.hopkinsmedicine.org/health/wellness-and-prevention/the-brain-gut-connection

4   Nick J. Spencer et al., Identification of a Rhythmic Firing Pattern in the Enteric Nervous System That Generates Rhythmic Electrical Activity in Smooth Muscle, *The Journal of Neuroscience* (2018).

5   Galland L. (2014). The Gut Microbiome and the Brain. *Journal of Medicinal Food*, 17(12), 1261–1272. https://doi.org/10.1089/jmf.2014.7000

ing your brain about potential stressors, rather than vice versa which is what most people believe. Sensations in our stomach or intestines (our gut-brain) alert us about danger and ways to interpret our surroundings. It tells us how to tap into the information that is being received, and it's on us to learn how to listen. This is the literal reason behind saying we have a *gut feeling*. In fact, listening to your gut instinct has been proven to help you make better decisions. Results from a Stanford study of logic-based (head) decisions versus intuition decision-making demonstrated that going with your gut led to the best outcomes 68 percent of the time. And this study involved people who hadn't even honed their intuition, such as those in business and finance careers. Even the US military uses intuition to help sense impending danger on the battlefield.[6]

The gut also signifies stressors through illness, like chronic digestive conditions. Seventy percent of patients with Crohn's disease and ulcerative colitis believe that symptoms of their disease are related to stressful events.[7] Medicine is now starting to use this gut-brain axis interaction as a viable treatment option for GI illnesses, and the influence of gut microbiota on human behavior is an exciting new topic of research.

The gut and the brain are closely connected, not only for proper GI function and intuitive decision-making but

---

6   https://www.nre.navy.mil/media-center/news-releases/more-feeling-onr-investigates-spidey-sense-sailors-and-marines

7   https://loyolamedicine.org/blog/how-your-brain-and-emotions-control-your-gut

also in the neuroscience of emotions and states of feeling.[8] As Emeran A. Mayer from the G. Oppenheimer Center for Neurobiology of Stress and Resilience puts it: "Recent neurobiological insights into this gut-brain crosstalk have revealed a complex, bidirectional communication system that not only ensures the proper maintenance of gastrointestinal homeostasis and digestion but is likely to have multiple effects on affect, motivation and higher cognitive functions, including intuitive decision making."[9]

It's no wonder that we hear signals from our gut as it is indeed sending us messages. There is an actual neurological basis when someone makes a decision based on their gut feeling. Those butterflies you feel in your stomach are, in fact, the neurotransmitters in your gut firing. And this intuitive decision-making can be honed and refined, if we want it to be.

I didn't always have the knowledge I do now about the power my intuition carries for the natural world. Fifteen years before being dropped off in the wilderness of Canada by a helicopter to survive on my own, I was a biology teacher who was diagnosed with multiple sclerosis (MS) and was completely unable to walk. In early 2000, at the age of thirty, I was diagnosed with this debilitating autoimmune disease after a previous diagnosis of optic neuritis, losing the eyesight in my left eye, which is a classic sign of MS. The clear white lesions doctors found in my brain

8   Mayer E. A. (2011). Gut feelings: the emerging biology of gut-brain communication. *Nature reviews. Neuroscience*, 12(8), 453–466. https://doi.org/10.1038/nrn3071

9   https://www.ncbi.nlm.nih.gov/labs/pmc/articles/PMC4010961/

from the stripped-away myelin sheath, the protective coating around my nerves, solidified my diagnosis.

Overwhelmed with the news, in shock and sadness, I followed my doctor's orders without question. My neurologist put me on an injectable drug for the illness, as well as drugs to combat muscle spasms, drugs to combat fatigue, drugs to combat the side effects of all those drugs. Never was I told about alternative therapies. Never was diet or lifestyle mentioned. Never. Alternative medicine was very alternative then, and so I went along with the program my doctors prescribed for me because I thought it was my only choice.

My symptoms only got worse, and my health continued in a downward spiral. I was facing life in a wheelchair and the complete deterioration of my mind and body. Two years later, I had to quit my job as a teacher because of my increasing physical disabilities. I used a cane during the day and often a wheelchair at night—and that was on the days I could get out of bed. My concentration and memory were shot. The left side of my body stopped working altogether. Sometimes a book was too heavy for me to pick up. I was a shadow of my former self.

A voice inside began to tell me something, and I began to listen. This was not living, and there *had to be* more options than the plan doctors had put me on. I needed to explore what healing looked like for me, specifically, and I knew once I found more answers, there was a good chance I could thrive again. This will not be the way my story ends, I told myself. It was time to take my life back.

Against my doctor's advice, I quit the daily injections. I decided that the psychological ramifications of taking multiple drugs and injections was like a daily reinforcement of what I was, not what I could become. The injections said *Stay sick*, and I knew I needed to stop telling myself that. With that drug gone I could then get off the drug I took to counteract its side effects. One by one, I was able to wean myself off the medications. Being a scientist, I delved into peer-reviewed research and studied herbs such as lion's mane, reishi, and turkey tail mushrooms as therapies. Little by little, with natural remedies and dietary and lifestyle changes, my body began to come back to me. Soon, not only could I walk again, I could run. My stamina, clarity, and vitality returned. And while I still have MS, it is no longer progressing, and I've had no new brain lesions develop since. I have my gut to thank for telling me there might be a different path toward self-healing. I switched neurologists to one who believes in holistic health—although now I only need to see him every few years for my confirmational MRI. Naysayers abound, but the proof is, as they say, in the pudding, and thankfully research science is now confirming what I discovered to be life-changing for me. Many others with autoimmune disorders follow my protocol, and they too are managing their conditions with great success.

My journey of healing took many forms. I manage MS successfully with an anti-inflammatory and wild-foods diet, herbal medicine (especially medicinal mushrooms, which are exceptionally effective in regulating the immune response, decreasing inflammation, mitigating the stress response, and producing neuroprotective effects), supplements, exercise, and lifestyle changes. Connective practices that foster intuition are the same practices that play a major role in keeping me healthy and strong.

My daily lifestyle regimen includes gratitude and mindfulness routines, which nurture the mind–body connection, nature connection practices, time away from media, and staying in the here and now as best I can. I feel well when I'm outside, but when I spend too much time in front of the computer or in town, I feel the symptoms of MS kicking back in again. I now live in a home in the woods where the trees, elk, deer, birds, and even the feel of the wind are all integral parts of my daily life—they are *my* medicine—but it took a lot of hard work and letting go to get here.

It can be scary to make intuitive changes to our lives because the result of that intuitive conclusion can upend our routines and comfort, and however hard our lives may be, that undoing can feel even harder. Our abandonment of intuition as an integral part of our daily lives is a profound generational loss, one that has been slowly disappearing and eroding over time. When I worked with the San Bushmen in the Kalahari Desert in Botswana, I got to witness the exact opposite—how intuition is a matter of survival and something to be cherished and nurtured every day. For them, it is something to be passed down, generation to generation. They are deeply connected to the states of their bodies and the earth around them. Intuitive communication is woven into their daily fabric of life. It is the norm, not a one-off special story. In their community, if intuition is lacking in someone it means that something is wrong: it's a sign of spiritual illness. Deep nature connection is a skill that has allowed our species to survive, and it is woven into our evolutionary past. Those early humans who didn't hone their intuitive intelligence did not survive—they starved or were eaten. It's *that* ingrained in each of us, present in our very DNA.

By experiencing firsthand how that community of San Bushmen lived, I know it takes real practice to cultivate a direct line to our intuition, and it took great lessons for me to get to where I am today. I've ignored the warning signs in the past, not just from my body but with my family, and have suffered great loss because I turned my back on what my intuition was trying to tell me.

A few years before I abruptly left that TV show, when I intuited my son needed me and was calling me back home, I missed the calling from another son, my eldest, Beau, who died in an accidental drowning.

In May of 2013, the day after I had given my commencement speech for my PhD, my phone rang. I had just stepped out of the shower when I saw the incoming call from Beau's dad, and I intuitively knew. In that instant, I knew something was wrong—I felt it deep in my bones. It was as if my phone lit up before it had even rung.

"Beau is missing," he said. I could feel something was very, very wrong, before he had even spoken. Yet yesterday, while giving my speech, I hadn't. My intuition was off by a day. How could I not have heard him? How could I hear one son and not the other? Why did my intuition fail? I was busy during his actual time of death, graduating with my late-in-life doctorate, and to this day, I feel that that ostensible noise was one large piece of why I didn't know, why I didn't hear his call.

After Beau died, I joined a grief-counseling group, and I spoke with other parents who'd lost children in sudden tragic accidents. They hadn't intuited their children's distress either. But I didn't understand how I, of all people, could not have known. I felt like I was a connected person—the type of person who would *know*. But I hadn't. Looking back, I realize I was in shock. After I got the news that Beau was missing, I quickly got on the last flight out of Phoenix to California...rushing to the airport...running to get on the flight...being the final, sweaty passenger as the doors shut behind me. Shock. Disbelief. Grief. Yes, grief already creeping in. Hope was still there, too, as I needed to have hope, but part of me already knew. I believe this is because my brain was trying to protect me by letting the truth in gradually—the truth that my oldest son was gone.

Almost a month later, after tirelessly working with the police, trackers, the coast guard, and a private investigator, we finally got our answer. Beau had drowned.

Perhaps there is another reason I wasn't tuned into his distress the way I thought I should have been. I have wondered if part of the reason I couldn't tune in was because I'd never had to perceive something like that before. Did that experience with Beau teach me how to hear my other son two years later when he called me home from Vancouver Island? Intuition is both innate *and* learned, and it takes practice to cultivate a direct line with it. The trauma, grief, and loss of one son may have been the experience I needed to be able to tap into what my gut feels like when my children are truly suffering. It may be part of why I heard my other son as clearly as if he'd been right there beside me in the woods.

There are plenty of reasons why we sometimes get it wrong with our intuition—and why we don't, or can't, listen. As modern-day humans, we are more tuned into verbal language that we can easily understand versus our intuitive language, which requires practice to tap into. We've been taught to prioritize words and our alphabetic languages over what is hard to put into words, what our gut needs us to hear. We may also put too much value on having a relationship, and thus become subdued by that need for codependence (e.g., the need of a relationship, need to be loved, accepted, etc.). These are powerful feelings, which can override our intuition. Animals are more disciplined than humans in this way. They have less noise and fewer extraneous distractions, so their judgment is not muddied in the way ours often is. They are purely instinctual, whereas we have been groomed by the modern world not to be. People often say that we are not animals. But we are animals. Tapping into our intuition doesn't make us less human, it allows us to tap into our full potential *as* humans.

For women, not listening to our intuition is often a product of societal constructs. We are raised and taught to be polite, and in our politeness our understanding of danger can be muted. Our intuition has been defanged and told that the wilderness outside and our wildness inside is not something we should value.

★ ★ ★

Intuition is something we can relearn and access; it is not unattainable and mystical. Given my training as a biologist, a scientist's logic was always my overriding go-to, so I had to learn to listen to my inner voice and cultivate how to hear it. Below are some tangible ways to harness your intuition and reconnect with the natural world.

- **Understand how intuition works uniquely for you**. Recognize that we don't all experience intuition in the same way. Some have a picture in their mind, some feel it in their body, some hear it as a story or words, some see silver lines leading to a place or a being. Each of us must develop an understanding of how intuition works for us uniquely.

- **Backtrack your intuition/write it down**. If you have an experience with intuition, verbalize it and journal it so that you can track your experience of how you saw/felt/heard the signal. Your inner voice may tell you that it was not real but your perception/sensation/subtle feeling was true. Name it so that you can better identify it the next time. For example, a few years ago I felt a mountain lion on the prowl. I called out to the two deer foraging in my pasture, "Careful tonight! There's a hungry cougar here." The next morning I woke up and found that this cougar had indeed killed a deer behind my home. This confirmation of my intuition helped reinforce that my gut feeling was correct and worth listening to.

• **Share your story**. Having someone to tell your story to who won't laugh at you or disregard you is very important. Remember, not everyone can catch your story. Find someone who will listen and understand. Telling it amplifies it and solidifies that it was real. In my experience, those who share their stories are better able to tap into their intuition in the future.

• **Don't brush off an intuitive feeling or a whisper in your head as irrational or wrong; surrender to it**. This gets easier with time and with success. Don't listen to your inner critic.

• **Practice and calibration**. We need to calibrate our intuition by practicing with things that are everyday (like finding your keys). Build your intuitive muscles much as an athlete builds her muscles through exercise.

• **Quality time in nature.** Go outside often and spend time in the outdoor elements (also called *dirt time*). This will help you become more connected to yourself, nature, and even others. See below for nature connection strategies.

• **Solo sit spot.** To become more connected, find a sit spot and go there alone without your phone. This is somewhere you go outside every day that is easy to get to: your front porch, your back deck, a local park. By going there daily you get to know every living thing that comes through the area and form a connection with them as individuals. By sitting in a sit spot each day you will recognize the slightest changes in the seasons and weather. I see when the maple leaves start to bud and, later in the year, start to fall. I know when I should start harvesting the stinging nettles and the huckleberries. Finding a sit spot and developing this type of connection can be done anywhere you live, even if you're in the city. Try adding a bird feeder to bring in more wildlife.

- **Quiet your mind and be in your body.** Meditate, give gratitude, turn off your devices, start your own sit spot practice.

- **Build relationships with individual animals versus species of animals**—like the squirrel or raven in your yard or the bears at my site on Vancouver Island—just as we do with our pets. *A sit spot helps with this.* On my land, I know the individual deer who forage here. I know that the mama deer just had twins. I know that one twin was recently eaten by a cougar. I know the bear that comes and climbs my apple trees. I know the pair of robins, and I found great joy in watching them build their nest. That nest was low enough I could see the eggs inside and then the young birds. I was saddened when a bigger bird came in and ate one of the eggs. Then a fledgling fell out of the nest, and one of the robin parents came in to defend it. Not only did the baby die but one of the parents died as well. I felt that pain along with the robin because I had developed an individual connection to it. I don't just know robins, I know *these* robins.

• **Stay in the now/present moment.** Being in the now opens you up to intuitive moments.

• **Timelessness.** The gift of timelessness seems nearly impossible to acquire, as it seems there's always a schedule to keep. When there's nothing pressing on the calendar, go for a walk without your phone or watch, and give yourself the incredible gift of timelessness. Looking at the time pulls you out of the present moment and puts your mind on what you need to do next.

• **Practice ancestral skills.** Learning wilderness living skills not only empowers people to go out in the woods and feel competent and capable, these skills bring people joy and lights them from within. You can do anything from weaving a basket to starting a fire for the first time without matches to tanning a deer hide to carving a piece of wood. Anything that takes you out of your headspace and puts you into your heart space works. Practicing these skills activates your primal brain. We've been engaging these skills for tens of thousands of years, and reestablishing them within yourself allows you to flex that genetic muscle memory. I teach at ancestral skills programs all across the country and in Canada. My kids have grown up going to these with me, and when we're at one of these programs, I look around and see people joined together around a campfire, talking and singing. They're joyful, connected, and fully alive. In these moments they are living happy, purposeful lives, and they are open to what the world—and their gut—is telling them.

- **Trust the feeling of body radar**. Trust that slight activation and pull in your gut. I use this when tracking wildlife. It works.

- **Be in service.** The greater the need, the better the results. Intuition works best if it has a need greater than yourself, like hearing your child call to you. Love is a powerful stimulator of intuition.

- **Notice if your body fills up with electricity.** The San Bushmen call this *num*.

- **Be playful.** Playing helps us stay in the present moment. It's not just for kids!

- **Take probiotics.** According to a study in the journal *Frontiers in Psychiatry*, beneficial gut bacteria have a positive effect on anxiety and mood due to the vagus nerve.

- **Deep breathing.** Activate that vagus nerve. It is a communication pathway between your gut bacteria and the brain. One way to increase vagal activity is to breathe deeply for several rounds in through your nose for four seconds, then exhale through your nose for eight seconds. Researchers found that this method increased vagal tone and improved decision-making when practiced for as little as two minutes.

• **Expose yourself to the cold.** When we experience cold temperatures, the vagus nerve is activated, and the fight-or-flight stress response is reduced. Options include cold showers, going outside in cold temperatures with minimal clothing, or dipping your face into icy water.

The question I was asked most after my time on the show *Alone* was *What was the hardest part of your journey?* People expect me to reply that being alone was the hardest part, or being hungry, or missing my kids. But it was the transition back into Western society. Once back, I had to figure out how to change my life so that I wasn't stuck in fight-or-flight mode, as many people are today. I had to learn how to block out the constant chatter and the never-ending visual and auditory stimulation. I had to find out how to chop wood, carry water while living not just in the woods on my own but in community with my family, technology, and the modern world. I moved to a house in the woods, where I can still take phone calls and emails but where I can also step outside into the quiet of nature every single day, anytime I need to. This, for me, is the perfect balance and allows for my mental and physical health to stay strong and for my intuitive life to thrive in the process.

Our society puts much emphasis on productivity. We

ask our kids and our partners, "What did you do today?" instead of "What did you experience today?" We seem to look at what is produced rather than the process itself. What if we shifted this to an emphasis on connectivity? Connection to self, connection to nature, connection to each other. Changing my mindset to be a connected force has shifted my life in a palpable, positive way, and I want that for you, too.

I hope that my stories and experiences will help you harness your own intuition through a deep reconnection to nature and your body. Take these lessons and stories that I have shared, and go out and give them to others, preferably around a campfire.

# There Are No Angels

*By Meredith Talusan*
*Writer and Cultural Critic*

My roommate from Craigslist said, "Welcome home!" the
first night I arrived in San Francisco from Boston and then
kissed me square on the mouth. I'd been desperate and re-
covering from my gender reassignment surgery, so I put
my deposit on a room on South Van Ness across the street
from a supermarket, sight unseen. It was late August 2002,
and I was about to start an MFA program at California College of the Arts with a focus on photography, a medium I
owed a debt to because it showed me who I was, a woman
and not a man, from the first time I trained a camera on
myself wearing a dress.

This roommate I'll call *Alex* because I don't remember
his real name (I don't want to remember his real name) must
have seen the shock and disgust on my face when he kissed
me, because I did feel both: the shock of the unwanted and
unprovoked intimacy, the disgust at the cigarette fumes in
his mouth and all over him.

Less than three months after medical transition, I was still in the early stages of being seen as desirable in my new gender, and I hadn't yet experienced a man's advances when he also had power over me. Alex was the primary tenant and controlled who was and wasn't allowed to live in the house, so I pretended like nothing had happened, even though I wanted to tell our three other roommates, all of whom were young women. But keeping quiet didn't make a difference. After two weeks, he confronted me in the hall outside his room and told me we weren't "vibing" and I needed to move out by the end of the month.

That was how I ended up a newly transitioned trans woman desperate for housing, somehow undeterred and answering roommate ads on Craigslist, a few from single men who requested pictures. It would take me years to register why some women prefer to only room with other women, never having done that in my life, having worked in an all-male-until-I-transitioned MIT lab immediately before taking my art school turn.

When people look at you, they only see the person you are now, and I presented myself as a confident young woman, so that was how people saw me. What people didn't see was the entire lifetime when I was raised as a boy and lived as a man, and I couldn't just leave all those years of social conditioning behind overnight. So it didn't yet register with me that what happened with Alex was something I needed to look out for in other men. Being new to womanhood, I still didn't know then how men could hurt me so deeply, even though they already had.

One of the men who answered my ad was named Joe,

and he invited me to meet him at a loft among the industrial buildings of SoMa, the neighborhood south of Market Street where industrial warehouses were only beginning to be turned into fancy lofts. The first thing I registered when I entered his space was his eighteen-foot ceilings and not the self-consciousness that came with being a young woman alone with a man at least a decade older and significantly bigger. Joe was bald and goateed, but silver-rim-spectacled in a way that suggested intriguing contrast.

I told him about my situation: artist, new San Francisco resident, asshole roommate who kissed me my first night in town and then kicked me out. He was a divorced Silicon Valley engineer with kids he saw on weekends who recently got licensed as a massage therapist while figuring out new business ideas.

"What does it mean on your email," he asked in a voice both raspy and kind, "that you're transgender?"

His question confused me. Did he not know what *transgender* meant? "I feel like I'm a different gender than I was at birth," I replied.

"So...you feel like you're a man?"

I had to laugh, out of amusement but also to cover being puzzled over his denseness, his denial. Maybe he thought it would flatter me, to be mistaken for female-at-birth.

"No," I replied, "I used to be a boy."

"I have a confession to make. I showed your picture to a friend, and we both agreed there's no way you couldn't be a woman."

"There isn't."

"Right, of course."

He changed the subject and told me he could work with my budget, even though it was only a third of the rent. He took me upstairs to the sleeping area, which was just one large open space with a ledge overlooking the rest of the loft. He explained that he would put up a wall and door, and I could decide which room would be mine. I said okay. Frankly, I didn't expect to find anything better as an openly trans woman with a cat and less than two weeks to move.

"We should get to know each other," he said.

I was used to being around men; getting to know my future roommate made sense.

"Of course," I replied.

Joe dropped by the apartment I was getting kicked out of in a navy blue pickup truck a couple of days later. We planned to go back to the loft and figure out which of my furniture to keep and how to fit the rest of my belongings in an apartment that didn't have much closet space.

In the bucket seat of his Ford, Joe asked me what I'd been up to, and I told him I went out on my first internet date in San Fran, but I probably wouldn't be seeing the guy again.

"He was boring," I said. "And hairy. He probably has too much back hair."

"That's too bad," he replied, in a way that made me blush because I didn't consider how Joe might have back hair himself or that, maybe, he cared about what kind of guys I liked. I dismissed the thought because he couldn't possibly, because only tranny chasers cared what I liked. Most men ran away once they knew I was trans or else demanded that I not tell anyone.

When we got to the loft, Joe made some tea while we talked about a massage retreat he was planning to run in Hawaii with a friend.

"By the way," he said casually as he grabbed a piece of paper from the kitchen counter, "here's a coupon for a free massage so you can refer me to your school friends."

I examined the sturdy, off-white paper with one of those stock massage images on it: a woman on her stomach with an anonymous pair of hands on her shoulders mid-knead. I imagined myself as that woman, supine on a massage table, and imagined Joe's hands on my own shoulders. I felt a surge of attraction, the way I'd fantasized about straight boys in college, guys on the crew team or that corn-silk-haired Mormon boy who told me he was like a painting in a museum: look but don't touch. Except now the no-touch rule was not because of the person but the situation.

I didn't really imagine being attracted to Joe as a problem, or maybe I did, but maybe it was a problem part of me wanted to have, having only seen messy romantic situations with roommates in Hollywood movies and not real life.

I took Joe up on his massage offer a week later, the night after we moved in my furniture. He set up his massage table in the living room of what I was beginning to think of as our loft, whose height stretched over two stories and was grand in a modern way I hadn't experienced before. Because the space was entirely open, Joe went inside the bathroom as I undressed, and I set myself stomach-down under the sheets.

"Ready?" Joe asked, his voice muffled yet somehow also resonant in that cavernous space.

I heard the door latch click a split second before I said *yes*.

Joe's hands were quickly upon me, and as soon as they were, I asked myself whether this was a good idea: maybe a massage implied an intimacy I shouldn't have and didn't want with my future roommate. Yet, he was a professional, certified, even dressed in the black shirt and loose pants that were the uniform of his trade. I relented and relaxed, and only tensed when he brushed the side of my breast a bit too close, a part of my body I still wasn't quite used to thinking of as my own. After a while, I gave in to the pleasure of his warm touch and his good hands and found it easy to ignore the small voice inside that wasn't so sure.

It was in this state of enjoyment and relief that I felt the shock of Joe's penis on my thigh, as he hovered over me to get to my back, and sensed both a persistent hardness and contact that lingered longer than it should have, even if the rest of him conducted business as usual like a masseur. I let the feeling pass, eager to dismiss it because this was a person I was now depending on for my housing.

"Do you want to try massaging me?" he asked after he was done. "I can guide you."

*Not really*, I wanted to say. "Okay," I said instead.

He went back to the bathroom while I dressed and took deep breaths, trying to push aside the thought that what had happened with my first roommate Alex only two weeks before was happening again. As I finished putting my blouse back on, my back turned away from the bathroom door instinctively for privacy, I wanted what was happening to feel like a normal massage. That was when I felt like someone was watching me, and when I turned around, I found Joe completely undressed, his penis erect.

"I don't mind being naked," he said. "I figure it would save us time."

The room felt too bright all of a sudden, the dozen track lights above us that illuminated the room in overlapping pools doing too good of a job. My body felt locked in place and time, unable to fathom what to do next. This was a feeling unknown to me since I had transitioned, as someone who was raised to possess autonomy over my body at all times, before I began to find myself in situations that felt as if a man wanted to own that body. I didn't yet know that Joe had made the massage coupon only for me, even though he made it seem like it was something he offered people all the time. I didn't yet understand that this must have been his plan all along, maybe from the moment we met, to live with me and take me to bed and whatever else he thought would happen afterward.

I would have stood in place forever—or until he left the room—if he didn't interpret my staying in place and lack of response as encouragement, and maybe that was what it became. I would have stood in place forever if he didn't come over and carry me in his arms, if he didn't take the cold metal stairs up to the bedroom where a wall had not been erected as promised, nor would it ever be. I would have stood in place forever if he had not deposited me softly into bed like a beloved pet, docile and unknowing, my systems only kicking in when he kissed me, because even though I knew so little about being a woman with a man,

I knew even less what to do in a situation when a man appears before a woman naked without warning. Before my transition, I had never been put in situations like this, given favors with ulterior motives attached. I had never had to read between the lines of a man telling me that the two of us should get to know each other better. I had never had to question the intentions of a so-called roommate. When I was young, no one expected me to grow up a woman, so no one—neither parents nor siblings nor friends—taught me these lessons or warning signs. The one thing I did know was how to give a man pleasure, even if I didn't yet know with my new body parts how to get pleasure in return.

Afterward, Joe and I lay in bed while he told me intimate details about his life. He'd felt trapped in his marriage and battled depression for years, which culminated in a series of suicide attempts the previous year, and the realization that he needed to leave his marriage if he had any chance of staying alive. He couldn't spend another day writing programs he didn't care about, and he had married too young for him to know what he really wanted.

This intimacy was more than I expected from someone who knew I was trans. My image of trans women in relationships up to that point, if they were in relationships at all, came from movies like *The Crying Game*, where the protagonist throws up after finding out his girlfriend is trans, or *Paris Is Burning*, where a trans woman is murdered after hiding her identity from her lover. That Joe got me into bed in circumstances I was ambivalent about, that he was clearly battling mental illness, did not ultimately prevent me from starting a relationship with him, because such a relationship was more than I felt like I should expect as a trans woman.

In late September, a month after Joe and I began to live and sleep together, we went to see the musical *Rent*, which had come into town on tour. A friend organized a group to see it, and Joe, being the straight engineer that he was, was completely unfamiliar with the show. I had the entire score memorized, since it was one of the few mainstream shows that portrayed queer relationships and so had become a favorite among my gay friends ever since it premiered on Broadway my senior year of college. As we held hands before the houselights went down, it occurred to me that I'd never seen *Rent* as a girl, even though I'd seen it several times as a boy.

We hardly talked during the performance because Joe was transfixed as I stole glances to watch his unblinking eyes, his slightly open mouth, his discovery that, being with me, he suddenly had access to a different point in social space, another orientation. I knew more about him by then, that he'd escaped a quotidian life in Silicon Valley with a wife and four kids. He had gone from suburbia to queer San Francisco, and I felt like a corner piece of the life puzzle he was trying to solve. I was the answer to his burn of bored desperation, everything seemingly past in the matte reflection of those stage lights on his unerringly muscular face.

Among the trans relationships that floated through my mind when Joe and I first got together, I'd forgotten about a character in *Rent* named Angel. Maybe I thought of her

as a drag queen rather than a trans woman back when I was
a gay man. She nurses the programmer–philosopher Colin
after he gets mugged, and the two of them begin a loving
relationship after Angel invites Colin to stay with her for a
while. Angel subsequently dies of AIDS, and in her funeral
scene, the other characters referred to her as *she* even though
they used *he* in the original production, which paralleled
my own shift in identity. Here was a relationship between
a man and a trans woman that was loving to the very end.

In bed after the show, I turned to look at Joe's face again,
this time in the shadow, barely distinguishable from the rest
of the darkness, in that room with just a sliver of a window.

"You're an angel," he said, and I wasn't sure if he meant
in general or the character.

"You're the one who saved me," I said.

"We saved each other. And I love you."

Was this what love felt like for a trans woman? This feeling of warmth and depth of validation, that someone can
know who you are, who you've been, and say those words
to you? That someone can love you the way you love yourself for being yourself? Someone virile and manly without
question, who proved his worth to the world as a being,
as a body who sired children? I had no way to distinguish
loving someone and being seen by them, being held precious, being taken as valued, as real.

*I'm not sure what love means*, I wanted to say. Instead, I said,
"I love you too."

Neither of us could sleep, so we took a ride on Joe's
BMW motorcycle for a spin across the Golden Gate Bridge,
which felt anticlimactic from the first time I saw pictures of

it: matte red instead of glowing yellow like in my imagination. But it felt like a climax that night, my arms around Joe out of need and a feeling of possession. He was mine, and I could be who I was with him and not be abandoned like I had been by parents, friends, and a previous partner who thought I was his soul mate until I told him my soul had a different gender. There was no abandoning anyone that night, just shelter in the warmth of Joe's back as I held on tight to his body and to the fantasy of being with a rugged man who loved me.

It was only a season, whatever love we shared. Joe grew withdrawn over the next few months and found himself attempting to take his own life again while I was on winter break in New York that December. His ex-wife's sixth sense saved him, and he spent a month in an institution where I visited often, all the while wondering whether what I thought of as his love for me had just been mania that whole time. I spoke to him on the phone the morning he was about to be released from the hospital, and he told me he needed time to think, so he wanted to be alone for the day. I wanted to give him space, unsure of my place in his life in a reality where we could be together and he could still want to kill himself.

I kept myself occupied and returned to the loft we shared in the evening but did not find him there. Still, my mind wanted to protect me from the possibility that something was wrong, even when I found the backpack he brought back from the hospital but no sign of Joe. The following afternoon, I came home from school to find police cars outside our building, and I still refused to believe that anything could be wrong. Joe's best friend, a police detective, had come to the loft to look for answers and found Joe in a storage unit, already dead. I didn't have his wife's sixth sense.

Because he died while I was very much a part of his life, and because that truth once made me believe it was partly my fault, and because my only consolation was the idea that I loved him and he loved me and that would be enough, Joe's place remained unexamined in my heart for a long time after he died. It took a lot of therapy to let go of my feelings of blame over not coming to the hospital when he was released, for ignoring that voice inside me that said I should, and for not being sure something was wrong as soon as I returned to our apartment and didn't find him there. I couldn't get myself to consider that our relationship itself might have been deeply wrong from the start.

Of the many hard stories to tell about that time, the easiest to tell—to others and to myself—was that I fell in love with my first boyfriend post transition and that he died.

I didn't get to see Joe after his death because his parents took his body to Indiana where I was not invited to the funeral because who was I to him? Not the woman who bore his children, nor the children themselves, just the transsexual who didn't even love him enough to watch out for the signs. And in the swirling mess of my emotions, all I could hold on to was my perception of the truth: that I loved a man and he loved me, and we would have kept loving each other if only things had been different.

Fifteen years later, after I moved to New York and started living with my eventual spouse, we were visiting my future in-laws in Connecticut for a long weekend when I sat down to breakfast and the *New York Times*. It was early in the morning, and I was alone. It must have been the fall of 2017, but I don't remember that. I don't remember much of anything, except that I read Harvey Weinstein's name and a description of him offering women massages to lure them into having sex with him. I remember my hands shaking so much that I dropped the paper. I remember starting to sob. I went to the bathroom and sat crouched in the toilet with my arms around my neck, like I was protecting myself from a bomb. I didn't want someone to find me so upset and ask me why. I didn't know why. Then I knew why. Joe.

If Harvey Weinstein had used his power to get women to sleep with him, what had Joe done to me? I did not want nor intend to sleep with him, and I told him so, yet he stood before me, naked, and I knew I would have been homeless without him. Why did I stay with him after? Why did I ignore and put away how it all began? Maybe I was protecting myself from the ramifications of a reality in which someone I thought I loved had also coerced me into sex, someone whose death I grieved for so long I must now also feel anger toward.

Coming to terms with what Joe did has meant reexamining one of the hardest periods of my life and realizing how much worse it was than I had thought, allowing myself to understand how the simple story of tragic love that existed in my mind couldn't come close to the complicated truth of reality: a man who held such a singular place in the story of my life had taken advantage of me, and I didn't even know it.

I'd been in other coercive situations with men between

Joe's death in 2002 and the #MeToo movement fifteen years later, and I wish I could say that I knew what to do, but my conscious knowledge and intuitive actions have had a way of diverging from each other. Gaining more experience as a woman and being around other women more often has certainly helped, but even when I consciously knew myself to be an empowered feminist, even when I'd read many books about sexual coercion and rape culture, there was, and maybe always will be, a part of me that doesn't consider myself enough of a woman because I'm trans. And because a deep part of my unconscious feels this way, a part of my self-esteem has always rested on catering to men's desires, which left me vulnerable to forms of sexual abuse I didn't recognize as such until it was too late.

My gut knows so much more now that it didn't before. It knows the first man I was in a relationship with after transition took advantage of his power over me to get me into bed. This is no longer a question in my life that I have to ask myself; it is a clear answer. I thought I loved him, but my gut knows now that I was not in a place in my life to understand what love between a man and a woman was supposed to look like. My gut understands that it isn't love if you have to be talked into it by your partner or your own thoughts. I likely would not have felt love for Joe if I'd had the tools to understand that staying with him after he lured me into sex was a way for me to unconsciously protect myself from the truth.

Since coming to terms with Joe's role in my life, a lot has helped me to feel less alone. It has helped immensely that an entire culture's focus has shifted to address systems of power that create pathways for men to get away with coercive behavior and is working to end it. I may not have known how to listen to my gut way back when I was in such a fragile and new place in my life as a young woman, but my intuition now—my *knowing*—about my past relationships and even my current ones, be they romantic or platonic, has grown and shifted because of all that I have been through.

The entire structure of our society is predicated on the power men have over women, and my story is only one of innumerable others. I understand this viscerally in large part because of my experience living across genders. I already knew this from books before #MeToo, but I now understand it not just in my mind but in my whole body. I also understand that it's only in the telling of these stories that women and nonbinary people can continue to deepen our relationship to our intuition and shine a glaring light on how power is distributed among genders in society, especially given how so many men have been socialized to use their power to take advantage of women and how women have been conditioned to let it happen.

Seeing my story so clearly in the stories of other women who had also been coerced by powerful men made something very clear to me. It is through our collective storytelling as women and nonbinary people—the sharing of what we have intuited and learned—that we can break the cycle and pattern of abuse. Because the more we speak out about the times we couldn't hear what our gut was telling us, the more we can teach others how to not be afraid to listen to their own.

# Harnessing Catastrophes

*By Dr. Dara Kass*
*Emergency Medicine Physician*

We start medical school wide-eyed and ready to learn. On the first day we are draped in short white coats, handed down dog-eared textbooks, and given brand-new stethoscopes, which hang around our necks like medals. We are granted a seat at a pungent anatomy table where we finally get to see inside a human body. We learn to ask questions and research answers, to get tested on medical facts, to learn about the body, but above all else, to listen to the body. We are grateful that each passing grade gets us closer to a career we love, one of taking care of real, live patients and saving lives: a career as a physician.

But the truth is becoming a good doctor requires more than just an education. It takes an instinct. It is one thing to be able to recognize the devastating diagnosis when lab work comes back, it is another to be able to deliver that news to a person whose life will be forever altered. You need to be able to read people—not just X-rays—making sure that what you are saying is being heard. You need to understand when to stop talking and just listen or when to let quiet fill a room. Eventually, you recognize this skill as your physician's gestalt. *Gestalt*, like all great Yiddish terms, evokes a feeling rooted in your gut. It is the recognition that things have come together—from places you can't describe—to finally make sense. And that sense often points you in a new and often unexpected direction.

Physician gestalt develops and grows as a product of your formal education, your lived experience, and your deep visceral gut. Physicians are trained first as generalists in medical school and then as specialists in residency. My residency was in emergency medicine, which meant that I was taught how to take care of any patient, with any problem, at any time. We used to say that emergency physicians are jacks-of-all-trades but masters of none. But, in fact, we are masters of quick thinking and getting to the point.

Patients arrive in the ER undifferentiated: they rarely come bearing a note that says *I am eighteen, missed my period, am likely pregnant, have terrible belly pain, passed out in the bathroom, and my ectopic pregnancy is ready to burst. Please call the OB-GYN and get me to the OR.* Instead, they are moaning on a stretcher, holding hands with a friend, afraid to look you in the eye, waiting to be seen, and praying their belly pain will go away. And it is your job, as you walk past that stretcher, to take a closer look, quickly lay hands on their belly, ask the nurse if their pregnancy test is back yet, and bump their case up to the top of the list of patients you have been running in your head.

As emergency physicians, we spend our whole careers fine-tuning our gestalt to be able to see a life-threatening emergency before that life is really on the line. Put simply, that may be as straightforward as realizing someone in front of you is subtly critically ill or is at risk for permanent injury, and you need to do something—right now—to address it.

Sometimes, that feeling happens when you look into a patient's eyes and realize he's not able to look back, leading you to wonder what is going on beneath the surface. Other times, it's when you use all your senses to monitor a patient after they receive a medication, looking for subtle signs indicating the medication is working. We learn to listen to the voice in the back of our head saying *Something is off. Figure it out while you still have time.* Often that voice gives you a head start, before things become dire, signaling that you need to act.

Studies have been done in emergency medicine that look at the comparison between physician gestalt and objective algorithms in diagnosing serious medical conditions, meaning, the difference between a physician's instincts and objective data. This includes a 2016 study in the *Annals of Family Medicine* that looked at physician instinct versus clinical decision based on medical knowledge and how both are used in finding a pulmonary embolism (PE), which is a clot in the lungs that can be life-threatening. It can also be hard to find and declare itself when a patient is very sick. It is one of our so-called can't-miss diagnoses in emergency medicine, meaning if you miss it, someone may die. This study, which combined a specific blood test with gestalt or an algorithm, found that while the decision rule was slightly better than gestalt, they were both very good at determining the presence or absence of a life-threatening clot in someone's lungs. In other words: intuition is real, and when properly used, it works.

My clinical gestalt—my instinct—triggers that voice in my head to speak up when I'm in the hospital and pressed against time to make a life-or-death decision. But it has also informed so much of who I am as a woman and a mom. I have often borrowed this skill in my personal life, foreseeing patterns and outcomes that seem to indicate things may be headed in the wrong direction. (Let's call it *mom's gestalt*.) It is the voice in my head that tells me our children need help before they even ask. And frequently, my personal and professional worlds intersect, in that I can identify when someone needs medical attention in my own family.

I have three children, and my youngest, Sammy, was born smaller than I had expected. At first, I did what I was told. I leaned on his doctors, breastfed him on demand, and gave him supplemental formula. When that didn't work, I started hearing that voice in my head. For me, whether in medicine or in my home, it always starts out as a small whisper, like someone is telling me an important secret in my ear, only it's my own voice speaking.

When I looked down at Sammy's newborn face, I heard the voice say *Are his eyes yellow, or is it just the light?* I looked closely and realized they were, in fact, yellow. The voice got louder. *Why can't he gain weight? Which organ isn't doing its job? Is there something wrong with his heart or his liver?* Once answers came, the voice quieted down. I had a whole new list of things to do.

Yes, his eyes were yellow, and it was because his liver

was failing. Sammy Kass, our baby, was sick and eventually we realized he was going to need a liver transplant. He was just under a year old when we started to prepare. The dual doctor-and-mom voice inside me told me that I was likely the right person to be his donor, and after several tests, sure enough, this fact was confirmed: I was a perfect match. On the eve of Sammy's second birthday, doctors at Columbia University Medical Center replaced his diseased liver with a piece of mine, and today Sammy is a happy and healthy nine-year-old kid, living a good life.

My connection to my gestalt—my gut—has gotten me through every kind of disaster and trauma, even the very worst in New York City. In 2001, I was just a third-year medical student in the emergency department at Kings County Hospital when the Twin Towers fell on 9/11. I vividly remember being thrust into all-hands-on-deck mode. At that point, my only instinct was to help wherever I could. Watching those with more experience than me jump into action, mobilizing resources and planning for the worst, was something imprinted on me for decades to come.

Because of the magnitude of the trauma of 9/11, all medical students were called to duty that day, helping doctors move stretchers and get the hospital ready for what would surely be a massive influx of patients to come in from the site of the crash. Even more devastatingly, the rush never came. Though if they had, we would have been ready.

A few years later, newly out of residency, I was working as a doctor on Staten Island when Hurricane Sandy hit our shores. The voice once again whispered in my ear,

*Emergency departments tend to be on the ground floor of hospitals, which is great for patient access but not so great for catastrophic flooding.* We sprang into action before the worst of Sandy had taken hold of New York, discharging any and all patients who could safely go home while moving the rest to higher ground. We sandbagged most exits and sat in wait for new patients. Unlike 9/11, patients did come, and it was because of the collective listening my colleagues and I did to our instincts and intuition that many who came in were saved that day, including those we moved to higher floors before a single raindrop had even fallen from the sky.

However, the biggest emergency I've experienced as a doctor was much more recent: the COVID-19 pandemic of 2020.

Word of a novel coronavirus in China had spread in December 2019, but I didn't really start paying attention until mid-January 2020 when we started screening travelers in the ER for signs of a respiratory illness.

I had lived through infectious disease outbreaks in the past, and none of them materially changed our lives. Initially, I expected the same of COVID. But by the end of February, I sensed something was different with this virus. The voice whispered in my ear, *It's coming. Get ready.* I listened.

At first, it manifested as my taking special precautions without any definitive reason for doing so. A patient, who had no travel history, would come in with a respiratory infection. *Could this be COVID?* I asked myself. I put an N95 mask on myself and began my exam. She didn't have the flu, and it was definitely a virus, but we didn't have capacity to test, so I just gave her supportive instructions and sent her home.

★ ★ ★

Before long, the first wave of COVID had hit New York City, and our hospital started seeing a bump in patients needing care for respiratory illness. Many of these patients could still stay at home and do a telemedicine visit, which helped keep them out of the ER, but I sensed things would not stay this simple or safe for long.

This new virus wasn't just a risk to patients, it was also a risk for health-care providers treating those patients. For the first time in my medical career, I had to consider the risk to me and my family. As we saw in China and Italy, before COVID had struck America, doctors and nurses were dying from the virus left and right, with high rates of transmission within families of those infected at work. *Sammy*, the voice inside me whispered. *You have to keep Sammy safe before this virus explodes everywhere.* Seven years after the liver transplant, my son was doing well, but he was absolutely considered high risk for infection or complications of COVID. I knew I had to act fast to protect him from what he could be exposed to, through me and my work in the emergency department.

Almost overnight, infections surged in the city, and emergency rooms were overwhelmed with patients struggling to survive. I was getting ready to go back to work in the ER in just a week, and I knew I had to do something to protect my family and do it fast. How could I protect myself at work and decontaminate myself at home? Do I move into the basement or out of the house? How will I know if I am exposed or even infected? There were so many questions and uncertainties in those early days.

I did what I do when I need to quiet the noise and let my instinct take over. I went to SoulCycle and rode a bike in a dark room. And at the end of the sweaty hour, I walked back home with my husband and said, "I know what to do."

"What?" he asked.

"We need to move the kids in with my parents, and you need to sleep in a different room. This thing is going to get very bad very quickly, and there is a high likelihood that I am going to get COVID. I don't want to infect anyone. We need to move them out of the house before I head into the ER. You can stay, but we need to be six feet apart. We will reevaluate things in a few weeks when we know more about this virus."

And that is what we did. I moved my kids in with my parents Friday, March 13, 2020. The next day I went to work in the ER. It was unlike anything I had ever seen. Patients were sick, and they were getting sicker, but given how contagious the virus was, we knew this was just the beginning. People came in awake with oxygen levels the lowest we'd ever seen before. We started treating each patient as if they could give us the virus. We pulled together as health-care workers do. We were all in this together. Techs, nurses, doctors from other services, the sense of solidarity was palpable all over the hospital and throughout the city.

On Monday, March 16, I started having muscle aches. I thought I was tired from the weekend of nonstop shifts. I picked up extra telemedicine shifts to decompress the volume and help people at home. On Tuesday, I lost my sense of taste, and by Wednesday a telemedicine patient on Zoom asked me about my cough. That night, I scheduled a telemedicine visit as a patient and told the doctor I probably had COVID. By the grace of God, I was able to get tested (something virtually unavailable to patients who didn't need hospitalization), and on Thursday, March 19, I found out I had COVID.

I took a deep breath. In fact, I took a lot of deep breaths. Some were just to check if I could still breathe. So many of my medical friends were finding out they also had COVID, and some were getting hospitalized. I was definitely afraid. But fortunately, I was only afraid for myself. My husband was in the clear, since we had been six feet apart since before my likely work exposure. My kids were safe, especially Sammy, because we had moved them to my parents' place in New Jersey. And I was okay, taking it one day at a time, facing this new virus now as a patient, not just a physician.

I had a symptomatic but mild course of COVID. I went back to work a couple of weeks later, just as NYC was in the worst of the pandemic. Fellow physicians were wearing garbage bags as personal protective equipment because there was a massive shortage, and I lost a physician friend to suicide. Those weeks were some of the toughest of my life, but through it all my family was safe. Which made all the difference.

The voice inside me that tells me when to act and how fast to do it, or when to make a hard decision, has helped me navigate some of the most critical moments in my life. It has helped me protect my family, my city, and my country. It has made me the fighter, the mother, the wife, the disaster-whisperer I am today.

I'm the woman telling you something vital, something you need to hear, something that could save your life or someone else's or my own. I say it in hospitals, or with my friends at dinner tables, or in front of an audience at conferences, or on the nightly news when I'm on as a guest, or while tucking my children into bed. I'm the one who leans in to myself, to hear what is being said, who trusts that voice more than any other, and who wants to share it with you, too.

# In the Mouth of the Wolf You Will Find It: On Dreams and Healing Trauma

## By Amber Tamblyn

Since childhood, I've kept a diligent record of my life and my dreams in journals and diaries. I've accumulated so many over the years, they've become an entire wall in my office.

My earliest journals were explorations in secret-keeping, donning tiny silver combination or key locks, which I always kept sealed, lest some parental unit learn of my *real* feelings for neighbor Jesse Nolan. I would hide the key to a diary in elaborate scavenger-hunt-style locations throughout the house, the likes of which Nicolas Cage would not even be able to crack. Or I would write the code to a journal's combination on a cinnamon gum wrapper, fold it up, and stick it in the shoe of a doll, then hang a sign around her neck that said DON'T *touch me!! Thanks in advance, Jasmine.*

As I got older, diaries turned into journals and their

style so too bloomed. Blue diaries with teddy bears and locks were replaced by velvet ones where white silk ribbons were hot glue-gunned on either side of its covers. Where the metal locks once said *Don't even THINK about it*, the easy-to-untie ribbons said *Think about it a little bit*. I slathered the journals with stickers of forlorn angels, shiny stars, and wolves. Always wolves. *Canis lupus* on everything, everywhere. It was the era of naming each journal—"Blue Heaven," "Copper Lobster"—and each name was written across its cover in elaborate silver or gold cursive.

I had a deep need to authenticate my reality, to show archival proof that my existence, my dreams, mattered and would live on far after I was gone. My interior and exterior lives—my dream life and my everyday life—were so valuable to me as a kid, I not only had to give each one its own page, I had to give those pages their own cover title. I was one Sanrio Surprises soft gel pen away from giving my journals their own ISBNs.

In my preteens, the journals I wrote in hit their own kind of prepubescence and began to take themselves even more seriously, both in interior style and cover design. Their pages no longer donned opaque images of wolves howling at moons, but instead, simple lined paper with fleurs-de-lis in each corner. Lighthearted crushes on Jesse Nolan in my elementary years turned into ten-page missed-connection love letters to the guy that picked up our trash on Thursdays or diatribes against ex–best friends who would become best friends again in a matter of days. I would stamp the covers of these journals with wax seals bearing my initials or elaborate gothic designs, as if what I wrote inside was an official tattletale to a king.

Through my teens, my journals grew more practical: composition and Mead three-ring spiral notebooks with various colors for covers—whatever I could get my hands on. I scrawled the covers with Nirvana lyrics or lines from ancient poems I thought I admired but probably didn't understand yet. This generation of journals also had names but they were far less Hans Christian Andersen and more Joan Didion. "The Summer of My Regrets" reads the title of one of them. Or simply "Amber's Notes on Daily Life." On the back cover of another, the words *Hi this is Max!!!!* is struck through with a thick black line from a marker in my handwriting, with two words written underneath his making the intrusion abundantly clear: *NEVER AGAIN.* Boys were strictly forbidden from touching my journals, and whatever Max did was in such direct violation that I had to make sure the record reflected it. Max may have fucked around, but he sure did find out.

Keeping record of my life became sparse in my twenties and thirties, and stories of imaginary loves and troubles were replaced with real ones, but one thing remains continually consistent throughout all of them: my dream world. Since I was a child, my dreams have been wild playgrounds flush with powerful imagery—imagery that has almost always included wolves or some kind of wilderness that I am either trying to protect myself from or hide away in.

In one dream, I am with my father in a high-rise building as an impending storm is headed our way. I can see the pitch-black clouds in the distance heading toward us.

A wolf appears and guides us to safety as waves begin to crash onto the building. In another one, I am at a high school party down the street from my parents' apartment in Santa Monica where I was born and raised, and everyone is drinking and dancing under a dark red light. A kid pulls out a gun and starts shooting. Large wolves the size of bears come rushing through a back door as chaos ensues. I am both terrified about the shooter and in awe of the size of these creatures. As one runs by, I grab on to its fur and hoist myself up on its massive back. It lets me. We rush out the door and down the street into the night where I can see kids running and screaming for their lives and hear the sound of sirens in the distance. In another, my mother's jewelry has been stolen (a very real trauma that happened to our family), and I am desperate to find the pieces. Someone says a wolf took them and went into the woods. I go after the wolf, deep into the forest, and can see the gemstones gleaming in the dark from within its mouth. I am both chasing after the wolf with my mother's jewelry and running away from my mother's pain. I am scared to be in the wilderness of my subconscious life and also happy to be away from my conscious one.

I am never the wolf in my dreams, but sometimes my closest friends are. *"We come to an area where a small waterfall has iced over on the road next to a cliff,"* one of my dream entries begins in a journal from 2014. *"The road is broken, and there is much deliberating as to the safest way to get over the frozen waterfall where the road continues. We discuss getting on the ice rocks and pulling ourselves up, but we see Mindy—who is now part wolf?—scratching and kicking the frozen ice where the cliff is. 'This life is just not for me,' she says. We all scream for her to stop, but she's like an animal trying to get a mouse or something caught underneath it. Eventually, we realize she's digging through the ice with her claws, so we try and help her, but our hands can't do what her paws can. She finally breaks through the ice, but it's a semifrozen dam, and water comes gushing out from underneath. We are engulfed in the freezing water which takes us over the edge of the cliff, and the last thing I see is Mindy's tail as she goes over."*

In Katherine May's *Wintering,* which explores winter as more than just a season but a period of time in anyone's life for self-nurturing and repair, she writes, "The wolf is part of our collective psyche. As elemental to our thinking as the sun and the moon... In the depths of our winters, we are all wolfish. We want in the archaic sense of the word, as if we are lacking something and need to absorb it in order to feel whole again." While wolves held much space in my psyche and their presence seemed to inevitably point toward something I should be seeing, not all of my dreams have felt like extensions of my intuition with some meaning waiting to be harvested. What dreams mean or don't mean is part of the reason why it's so important to be in tune with them, to look for the real clues when they arise. "The old one, The One Who Knows, is within us," writes Clarissa Pinkola Estés. "She thrives in the deepest soul-psyche of women, the ancient and vital Wild Self. Her home is that place in time where the spirit of women and the spirit of wolf meet—the place where mind and instincts mingle, where a woman's deep life funds her mundane life."

Scholars and philosophers agree with Estés that our dreams and waking lives are inextricably linked, and whether one has something to tell us or not depends on how we choose to listen. Where depth psychologist Carl Jung believed that our dreams show us what is to come in the future, his mentor, Sigmund Freud, believed our dreams might reflect what has taken place in the past. One cannot help but be informed by the other and vice versa. Both agreed that dreams are deep reflections and manifestations of our unconscious mind, and that if intuited from, they can be a great resource for healing anything from mental illness to early childhood traumas. Estés writes that a woman's dream life is to be nurtured, cherished, and taken seriously, and that from it, we can reimagine ourselves in a freeing, new way. "Bone by bone, hair by hair, Wild Woman comes back. Through night dreams, through events, half understood and half remembered."

In a journal entry around the age of eight, I wrote about an event in my life, half-understood, half-remembered. It came to me in the form of a recurring dream very much tied to a real-life event that took place around the same time, though it would take me years to come to terms with it. I could recall most of what happened during the real event, but there were still many details lost out there, somewhere in the woods alongside the wolf with the jewels in its mouth.

The recurring dream and the event begin the same: I am lying in my parents' bed trying to sleep when their white wicker pendant lamp that hangs above a desk is turned on to a dim light. From here, the dream and the real event part ways. In the dream, someone who is not supposed to be in the room is coming in or has just left, and though I can't see them, I can sense their presence. Wolves begin to howl in the distance outside my parents' window—a sound which is always protective and comforting in my dreams. The sound has always symbolized a shift taking place, signaling a listening that has begun. The door to the hallway is halfway open, and I can see the blackness of the living room as I wait for the someone who is there, but not there, to emerge from the shadows. The wolves have gotten closer, and soon they enter the endarkened living room. I can hear their panting and frantic sniffing giving way to snarling and the sounds of someone being attacked—the someone who was perhaps here, in this room—a man, screaming. He cries out something in his own defense, but I cannot make it out. I go down under the blankets to hide and am both terrified and relieved. I feel protected and yet, somehow, preyed upon.

There are records of various versions of this dream in six of my journals, captured in over thirty different entries. At the time, I could not see any significance in their repetition. But as I grew older, I began to see them as breadcrumbs from my intuition—a path my body and my memory were trying to lead me down in order to discover something new about their significance. So I followed.

There was a young man named Matt who sometimes babysat me when I was younger. Matt was a teenager who lived in our apartment building complex and who was on the autism spectrum. He continued living with his mom for a while even after he became an adult, and he was always a reliable and kind presence in the building's courtyard whenever anyone ran into him. In fact, his only fault seemed to be that once he got your ear, he would never stop talking. I would often go to sleep in my parents' bed and wake up drowsy to the sensation of my dad picking me up and moving me into my own bed in another room. One night when Matt was babysitting me, I was woken up by the light of the wicker light being turned on low, but it wasn't my dad coming into the room. It was Matt. In the days that followed, I recounted how he had come to tuck me in a second time, a strange gesture toward a child who was already asleep. But my recurring dream of the dimmed lighting and the dark living room and the man being ripped apart by wolves, and the many iterations of this dream that manifested throughout the years that followed, brought new questions about the real story that mirrored it. The more I listened to what my intuition was telling me, the closer I got to the emergence of new details. Something was telling me to look closer, go in deeper, unveil, but the first reaction of my mind was to protect me from whatever might be illuminated; it was probably a story I did not want or need to hear. Knowing the latter was scared of the former, I knew I was onto something, and so I allowed myself to open that window inside me wider and listen for what wanted to be heard.

I worked with my therapist Evan for years on the meaning of those dreams and what had happened and let them help guide me in a direction that would give both the real memory and the dream memory some kind of closure. When I look back at the sequence of those dreams written out in such detail throughout my journals, I see a very purposeful unfolding, each informing the next, adding a detail here and there, like one frame of a film at a time. The wolves are far away. The wolves get closer. The wolves kill. The wolves enter my room, lick me, swarm around my bed smelling and sniffing with concern. The someone is in the dark of the other room, and then the someone who is not there suddenly is. The dream evolves into the real memory, awakened into revelation. The someone in the room was always Matt.

When Matt entered my parents' room the night he was babysitting me, I was around the age of eight. He sat by me on the bed. He did not tuck me in, but instead pulled the covers down. I was groggy and confused. He began to tickle me. On my ribs, my stomach, and my hips. I pretended to laugh, to play along. Then I told him to stop, but he wouldn't. Eventually he did and then got up to leave, turning the light back off on his way out. The recurring dream I wrote down in my journals was almost like a protection spell, obscuring parts of the real experience while leaving clues of what was true. The dream's ending always mirrored what really took place that night: *I go down under the blankets to hide and am both terrified and relieved. I feel protected and yet, somehow, preyed upon.*

The story was as simple and as complicated as that. When I was just a young child, a man I knew and trusted came into my room in the night and tickled me out of sleep and then left. It's possible that something else happened, something more disturbing that my mind still protects me from to this day, but whether or not that's true, the story as-is was enough. It was enough at the time because I told my mom right after it had happened, something I had blocked from my memory until years later while working with Evan. It was enough to subconsciously inform parts of my intimate life and some aspects of my relationship to boundaries and touch. It had affected me in ways I had not even been aware of. "Developing a relationship with the wildish nature is an essential part of women's individuation," writes Estés on the natural predator of the psyche. "In order to accomplish this, a woman must go into the dark, but at the same time she must not be irreparably trapped, captured, or killed on her way there or back."

Our dreams can mean nothing at all, or they can be responsible for huge parts of our self-discovery and healing. It is up to us to pay attention to which ones are which—which dreams are just doing a load of subconscious laundry, and which might be unfolding a truth. "Our dreams are continually saying things beyond our conscious comprehension," wrote Carl Jung on the matter. "We have intimations and intuitions from unknown sources. Fears, moods, plans, and hopes come to us with no visible causation. These concrete experiences are at the bottom of our feeling that we know ourselves very little; at the bottom, too, of the painful conjecture that we might have surprises in store for ourselves."

You can be afraid of the surprises—of the secrets your story might hold, however painful. But don't shy away from bringing them to light. What our subconscious intuits is not meant to be background noise. The radical change you seek, in your career, in your marriage, with your child, or in the world might be found there. Our dreams can be the great healers we've been looking for, giving us just the right dosage of what we can handle, when we can handle it; they can help us understand what we weren't previously ready to. As Katherine May puts it in *Wintering*, "Sleep is not a dead space, but a doorway." Dreams can inform our desires, our longings, our greatest life's calling. They can signal huge shifts coming down the road or open our creative lives up to groundbreaking ideas.

The stories in our dreams are direct lines to our authenticity: to the rawest elements of our emotional status, to the many varied states of our well-being. They are filled with potential, containers holding our most radical and revolutionary possibilities, each one waiting to be opened. Our intuition can be born anew from our dream life and catapult us into our destinies, one metaphor at a time, one awakening after another.

*Every night I have a dream that I remember the next day. Why do I have to always remember my dreams? Why can't I forget? I am secretly an animal, this much I know. I am always the same animal, every night, hunting in a different darkness.*

—Journal entry, May 1994

*Later, I am helping someone give birth. She is very scared. They are using forceps and I am helping her breathe. I am me and I am her. I am both the one giving birth, and the one coming out. On the TV in the background, rescuers are baffled by half a tiger they rescued, which is still alive despite having no torso.*

—Dream entry, January 2014

# LETTER TO OUR CHILDHOOD DREAMS

*Poem by Amber Tamblyn*

Authorities and the staff at the zoo are baffled
by the animal cut completely in two at the torso,
its lower half unmoving and deceased. The upper half

of my body washes up on a beach
right next to my mother's stolen jewelry.
*There you are,* I whisper,
my fur covered in the coffins of oysters,
fangs gnawing at the clutched cubes of rubies drizzled in
the sand.

*I dream of wolves,* I say.
I will grow up to be a wolf, I dream.

I will grow up to be a maze, not a labyrinth.
I will grow up to be a parallel sun, scorching fire
through all the masses of masculinity.
I will grow up to be a success story
read to your children at night.
I will win all the awards.
I will grow up to be every weapon on the market:
Dangerous. Callous. Ruthless. Unladylike.
Ambitious. Cruel. Ugly on the inside and out.

I will grow up to dream like the dreams of men,
to daydream of them, what they expect
from wolves like me.

I will grow up to be a man's wife.
I will grow up to have an affair
with a man's wife.
I will get pregnant with her child.
All the men will be so confused.
*It's a wolf thing*, we'll say.

I can breastfeed with my eyes.
What can you do, men?

War?
Good for you and your wars.

We own the moon.
What the fuck do *you* own?

I will dream my worst fears all run into rivers
of my father's remaining years.
He will be reborn an ocean.
I'll remember all that I've lost
and all that's been found
in his waves.

*Crash*

My father at the front door

trying to protect me from a white buffalo
with shards of glass for fur.

*Crash*

My father in the subway tunnel laughing
at the light headed straight toward us.

*Crash*

My father on the cliff. Trapped in the glacier.
Hanging on to the skyscraper.
Hanging out at the apocalypse.

*Please don't kill my father*, I say.
My father is always killed, I dream.

I will grow up to be a little girl forever.
I will grow up to be unafraid of my father's ending.
I will grow up to understand
that the weavings of my dreams
are not real,
until a single thread
undoes itself.

You might wonder why I don't bother to mention my
mother in this letter. I will address that later. Did you think
this was a poem, dear reader? I will address that later. You
probably wonder how I carry all my books, my dynamite,
my threats,

my swords, my venom, my brass-knuckle-patterned pant-
suit and all of my endangered pet panthers in this tiny purse.
I'll address that later.

*I will grow up to remain a little girl*, I say.
I grow up to become a child, I dream.

Or maybe
Maybe

Maybe I will grow up to stay alone.

Maybe I will have lived the wrong life.
I will have kissed too many magicless mouths.
I will have not done everything I could
to obtain good seats to an Adele concert.
I will be afraid I was never a wolf.

Are you afraid you were never a wolf?

Are you lost between the you that is them
and the you that is true?
Are you afraid of what will gleam back?
When you grow up, will you stand quiet
while rising temperatures tighten their grip
around the world's lungs,
or will the white you
stand quiet
as injustice reins?
When you grow up,

will you be complacent
or complicit?
Will you howl then?
Will you travel in packs and feed the hungry muzzles
of other women like you?
Will you or won't you?
Will you be a better actress than all the liars that came be-
fore you?
Will you return all the dresses you've stolen
from the mind of the man who doesn't love you?
Are you an object?
Are you thirty years old and completely lost?
Are you younger and completely lost?
Are you a wise woman and completely lost?
Are you completely lost with your shit together?
Completely lost and reborn?
Are you a completely lost priest? Or writer? Or veterinarian?
Are you even a woman yet?
Are you sure you're a wolf?
Are you as scared as I am?
Do you want to be loved deeper than the language
of what you've been given?
Do you want to be understood?
Are all our mothers disappearing inside of us?
Can I cry with you now?
Will you think less of me?

In my dreams and in my life,
my mother is the only wolf.

Hear me.
My mother
is the only
wolf.

Through her soft jaw I slipped into life,
a puddle of marble, drenching my father's hands.

*I am the only animal*, my mother screamed.
All the animals come out of the woods, she dreams.

All the animals except for one,
and the doctors are baffled
authorities are baffled
the White House is baffled
the zoo staff is baffled
pianists are baffled
eyewitnesses are baffled
Tom Brokaw is baffled
all your sons are baffled
by the animal cut in two at the torso,
its lower half unmoving and deceased, the upper half

of my body washes up on a beach
right next to my mother's stolen jewelry.
I cradle them just as she cradled me,
each stone, a daughter
that will someday
leave.

I let it all go out into the water,
my father, the sea;
my mother,
the wolf.

*There you are*, I whisper
to the dark that's been waiting
for me to become it.

*Here I am*, it whispers back.

# Two Worlds Are Better than One: On Dreams

*By Ada Limón*
*United States Poet Laureate*

One evening in Lexington, Kentucky, I woke to the sound of a familiar voice ringing out in my bedroom in the middle of the night. The room is cold and dark, only a hazy bar of light coming from under the bedroom door. No shadows. The sound of a clunky fan going round and round. I feel my heart muscles contracting quickly and powerfully, a squeeze and release inside the cage of the body.

Outside it's not yet morning, no glow on the horizon, just the streetlight doing nothing but lowering its metal head toward the pavement, fixed to its position, reporting for duty. My husband is beside me, his deep, slow breaths rhythmic and hypnotic. Nothing is disturbed. Even the dog is still burrowed in the pillows, only one eye open, watching me stir. The voice I heard in the night, of course, was me, my own raspy yell that broke through the dream world into the waking one as I screamed out, "You cannot take me."

Once my body calmed down, I was able to get up, pee, pet the cat curled in her bed underneath the nightlight in the bathroom, sip some water, and slide back into bed. My dog continued eyeing my movements, with the hope that the night was still the night and there was still plenty of sleeping to do. As I ease into sleep again, I unravel the dream I just had, pull the thread in a quilt of images, and try to hold on to something taking shape, like a fish slowly coming to the surface of a deep and murky pond. I want to find out its importance, what it was that woke me—what it is the dream is trying to tell me.

In the early 2000s I lived in Brooklyn and for a short time sang in a band named after my first book, *Lucky Wreck*. We played places like Pete's Candy Store and Spike Hill with moody southern-inspired singer-songwriter tunes that were all about heartbreak and longing. The guitarist and co-songwriter was from Alabama and had a thick southern drawl and an obsession with Burt Reynolds. He was also a licensed therapist. He once told me that it's not so much the content of the dream that requires analysis but the feelings of the dream itself—that there's a connection between the emotion you have in a dream and whatever you're processing in your waking life. That makes sense to me, but still, I'm interested in the images, too: the elemental factors that inhabit my dream life, the intense colors, the exact pieces of dialogue. For example, if I woke up screaming, I want to know *Who was I fighting?* I think dreams are more than the leftover emotions of the waking life, an entirely other world opening to us, allowing us to witness another life that requires just as much attention.

I was an active dreamer even at a young age. I could recall my dreams as easily as I could recall a memory from the day before. Most dreams I had as a child, growing up in Northern California in a pale green house off Arnold Drive, were about water. I grew up in Glen Ellen, and across the street from my house was a small creek called the Calabazas Creek that runs from the Mayacamas Mountains down to the Valley of the Moon and all the way to Agua Caliente, where it finally empties out into the Sonoma Creek. The stream is only five and a half miles long, but it runs heavy and long through my dream world. It did as a child, and it does now.

Just last night, the creek appeared as a clear, wide river full of luminous underwater creatures, including two snakes my husband had to fight. Once, the creek held an underwater cave that was full of sacred bones and ancient etchings on the walls. In my waking life as a child, I'd play in that creek for hours. It was where silence happened. At the center of the creek were large rocks I could lie on and watch the oak trees and toyon bristle in the wind. The creek was where I could escape doing and just be. It was a place for solitude. If there is one defining symbol in all of my dreams, it is the Calabazas Creek. Something that helps me remember my dreams now is the mantra *Where was the water?*

★ ★ ★

When I was about six years old, my parents got divorced, and I dreamed that the Calabazas Creek was on a fault line—I was on one side of it, and my whole family was on the other. An earthquake shook the clay-colored earth, and the stream widened into a huge chasm that separated us. I was left isolated from them, trying to reach them. Even now, I can still remember the force of that dream: the red clay rising up, the clear, high water, the low oaks breaking from their roots and falling into the creek. My family, disconnected by a giant fracture in the earth between us. As a child, I thought divorce meant being separated from your family forever, and my dreams were clarifying that for me. My own terrified heart made the earth itself crack open in my dream life.

I have always known that my dreams were not just dreams. Some were warnings, some were omens, some were ways of preparing the body and the mind for some unknown future to come, but they weren't something to be taken lightly. There is very little I can offer by way of explanation about this, but my dreams don't feel like remnants of the day's blitzed-out brain emptying its chaotic thoughts into the swirling crystal ball of night. Dreams, to me, feel like something organized, cinematic, epic, and as real as this world.

There are times when I do not know if I have experienced something or dreamed it. After all, isn't dreaming a way of experiencing? When I wake up in the morning, I write my dreams down, and they help me assess my current human predicament. I see what I'm up against. For example, I know if the water is clear, then I am on the right path. If the water is murky or full of monsters, I am contending with something and should pay attention to what's coming.

There is a meditation I do that is about trusting your intuition, tuning in to what it is that your whole selfhood is requiring. Each time I close my eyes and do the meditation, the very first thing that arises in my mind are images from my dreams. Dreams are how I figure out what I'm working on in the blood. Dreams are how I know if what I'm doing, the path I'm on, the choices I'm making, are right.

If life is a series of stories we tell ourselves, some more complex than others, and if we honor the fact that stories and storytelling are essential human traits, dreams should be included in our personal narratives. Joan Didion once said, "We tell ourselves stories in order to live," and like Didion, I believe a dream is a story we unconsciously tell ourselves in order to confront ourselves. It's not about making sense of something. It's about expanding the human possibilities of experience. Perhaps, like the Calabazas Creek, a story trickles from my mind and tells it to my body, then it flows from my body into my future reality. According to the philosopher and political theorist Hannah Arendt, "Storytelling reveals meaning without committing the error of defining it." We don't have to necessarily dissect our dreams to learn from them. Each dream is enough on its own.

★ ★ ★

Dreams are also a way that I connect with the past. Whatever past that is—generational, cellular, archetypal. My dreams don't always make me sure of a truth or give me all the answers. But they do carry lessons, and it's my responsibility to pay attention.

As I was getting ready to graduate college, I had a dream that I was part of a tribe that had been slaughtered. In the dream, I came out of my sleeping area that was made of hides and heavy blankets and found most of my family and tribe had been killed. There was snow on the ground, or ash, but either way, I could see the large footprints of a wolf. When I rounded the corner, I came face-to-face with a massive gray wolf, as large as a horse. He had blood dripping from his teeth. It was unclear if he was responsible for the deaths. He seemed neither benevolent nor evil. As I sobbed, he said very slowly, "It's your job to carry this." He was not mournful or ashamed, just matter-of-fact.

With his words circling inside me, I awoke, out of breath, my heart pounding. I've heard and honor the stories of generational trauma showing up on a cellular level, and though I'm not sure I believe in past lives, I cannot deny some of the vivid details of this dream. My native roots trace back to the Purépecha tribe in a region of Michoacán, Mexico, and though it does not snow there, they do have gray wolves. This was not a memory, and yet, I remember it, to this day, as if it were true.

* ★ *

The dream came at a time in my life when I had to make some big decisions. My path had been like the Calabazas Creek, and now it was bifurcating into two streams, one of which I had to choose: stick with my current passion as a performing artist in theater or become a writer. My undergraduate degree was in drama, and everyone I knew was going on to explore a life on the stage. I was taking an advanced poetry workshop and kept being pulled toward my own fascination of putting words down on the page.

I woke up from that dream, in my small studio apartment in Seattle, and wrote it down. I wrote down what the wolf said. It was my job to carry it. And whether I knew it then or not, I know now that my dream informed my decision to become a writer. And while that sounds absurd and exactly like the kind of thing a writer would say—"I became a writer because a giant wolf visited me in a dream!"—it remains a truth. My truth. The dream intuited who I was going to become before I ever did.

I trust that image of him, the wolf with his bloody fangs, the enormous, furred body. I trust the image of him standing amid the carnage in the snow more than I trust memories of some seminal college experiences. In my dreams, there is often water and sometimes there are wolves, but more frequently there is something to learn from, to turn over in the mind, interrogate, and pay close attention to. Joseph Campbell wrote, "Myths are public dreams, dreams are private myths." The myths that I make nightly in my sleep belong to the essential part of me that is more connected to the universe, the self beyond the self.

Six years ago, my life seemed at a standstill as I faced a strange, undiagnosable health crisis. I was struggling with vestibular neuritis, or vertigo, and while I received MRIs and constant medical advice, no one could figure out what was going on with my body. My blood pressure soared, my sinuses ached, I had constant fatigue, my back pain was unmanageable. Everything was off. But the worst of it was the dizziness. I couldn't write. Everything made me want to lie down or cry or give up. It was as low as I can remember being because even if I could see my way out mentally, I couldn't see my way out physically.

During this time, I couldn't find my way into my poems. I tried to write, but only poems about dizziness or nausea came. It was then I came up with the idea to write about my dreams, to connect my writing life with my dream life. I'd try to write one poem every day, and the job was to record the dreams with complete fidelity to the truth of them, the facts of them, while making the descriptions as poetic as possible. I wrote over forty dream poems, and with each revealing image, I found myself coming back to life.

In one dream, I could see the apocalypse coming, fire and magma ravaging the Mayacamas, and I was on the mountain trying to make my garden. There were flowers everywhere and hummingbirds. I remember the manzanita trees and bay laurel, maroon and red, vibrant on the hillside. I raked and raked in the black soil. I could see the volcano erupting. I knew it was coming, and there I was, insistent on making a garden. I woke up from that dream knowing that I wanted to try to have a child. Even if the world was ending, I wanted to give it a go. The most apocalyptic dreams I had, by far, were when we were trying to conceive.

When I stopped trying to have a child, for the most part the apocalyptic dreams stopped, too. In retrospect, after going through fertility treatments and finally deciding to stop trying, I think the dreams were giving me fertile ground, but they weren't telling me what I was going to make. Now I think they were also about making art, making a life, making love, survival. I also know that, deep down, part of the decision to stop trying to conceive was linked to the worsening climate crisis. My unconscious wanted me to see the world on fire.

The dream poems were strange, and certainly not all of them were good, but they were a window into me when I needed a way in. In one dream, my now husband wanted to catch a whale shark to prove how much he loved me. A teenager dressed like Holden Caulfield said that there was an inland fishing hole stocked with dragons, and it was easy fishing. I thought my husband should just go catch a dragon. Keep things simple. Instead, he wanted to go out on a big boat and catch a big thing. And right as the boat was hitting open water, an enormous whale broke the surface of the water and stared at us. I still remember the eye, the look. The animal watching us, the great eye of the world.

To me, this was a dream about the passage of time. We were busy proving ourselves, working constantly in our hectic lives, and we were missing out on the simple pleasures of life. The dream was telling me that time itself was passing us. The dream wanted us to slow down, stop trying so hard. The whale wasn't the wolf, but it was a warning, the idea of what is sacred, what can't be proven or caught.

In another dream poem, a crocodile caused a flesh wound on my thigh. In another, a single friend in leather pants leaned in and said, "You're a real person now," because I was in a relationship and no longer single. Sometimes in my dreams, the animals were ominous, sometimes the men were ominous, sometimes I was invincible, sometimes the whole world was coming to an end. All of these things were in my dreams. I recorded them diligently for forty days. Or rather, forty nights. And at a time when I could barely move my body to walk to the corner deli for toilet paper, I could travel whole worlds in my dreams. Night by night, I was living again.

Some say that you are every character in your own dream. That means I'd be my husband or the whale or the wolf or even the water in my dreams, but I'm not sure if I entirely adhere to that line of thinking. I do believe in archetypes. The elements and how they move through us.

Freud famously said that dreams are "concealed realizations of repressed desires," and I wonder what he'd say about the wolf dream, the great eye of the whale. Those aren't repressed desires; instead, they feel more like important and intimate images there to teach me something.

A few years ago, I was asked to apply for a prestigious academic job. Up until then, I'd tried my best to live on the edge as an artist. Though I'm on the faculty for a low residency master of fine arts program, I had yet to seek out or commit to a tenured track position. But the job was tempting. I made it to the last round of four finalists. I was honored and excited about the possibility of being chosen, but also I kept having terrible stomach aches and nausea when I thought about the permanence of the position. During this time, I dreamed that I was lying by a huge, beautiful pool surrounded by terra-cotta pillars and sandstone buildings. It was lush and golden, everything the color of sunset. Then, the director of the program suddenly appeared, and I realized that I was only there to clean the pool, not to lounge by it. I was reprimanded. I sat up, apologized profusely, and ashamedly began to clean the pool.

Shortly after this dream, I learned I didn't get the job. I knew it was for the best—every part of me didn't want it in the way I should. What might have seemed like freedom was ultimately going to sign me up for a lifetime of hierarchical bureaucracy. I thought the job would've been lying in the sun with the whole world glowing in pinks. But my dream—my intuition—knew the truth was I would just be cleaning someone else's pool.

If Carl Jung describes dreams as "a little hidden door in the innermost and most secret recesses of the soul," then I want very much for that door to be left unlocked. I trust what my dreams tell me, where they are guiding me. I want that hidden door to not be hidden at all. Because behind that door is a whole world of stories worth paying attention to. Sometimes they are the stories of what I'm truly scared of, and sometimes they are stories pointing me toward a future I didn't know was possible. If I'm paying attention to my dreams, I am paying attention to my whole life—the seen and the unseen.

In the dream where I woke up screaming that night in Lexington, I was telling someone they could not take me. When I stared at the dark circling fan for a while, I let the meaning reveal itself to me. I remembered someone trying to pull me away, to take me into the shadows for good, and I was having none of it. My husband once said, "Dream Ada is a fighter." And she is. Or I am. Or we are. If my dreams are my personal myths, then the myths, even the frightening ones, are essential to the organization of my inner life.

When I woke myself up, staring at that streetlight hanging its head down low, I remember thinking how strange the waking world was, too. The streetlight, the yellowness of human-made illumination. To me, the waking world and the dream world aren't so different, aren't so separate. They are both full of signs, full of stories that help me make sense of who I am and where I belong. They are my intuition.

I would resist anyone pulling me into either of the worlds permanently: I belong to both. Like the fish who rises to the surface, and the fish insistent on going deeper into the dark.

# The Field

*By Bonnie Tamblyn*
*Mother and Mentor*

---

*Out beyond ideas of wrongdoing and rightdoing, there is a field.*
*I'll meet you there. When the soul lies down in that grass, the*
*world is too full to talk about.*

—**Rumi**

Come, my children, and I will tell you a story of deep listening, of our connections to our instinct and the roots we all share as humans. It is our gift of cognition and recognition; that moment when something stirs inside and strikes us as different—notable, time out of time. We are instinctive creatures, after all. The companion to our instinct is our intuition, and the companion to our intuition, if we but heed it, is attunement—a deep listening to our shared story, the moment when we meet out in that field with a heightened sense of place, self, and other.

It's a chilly dawn in 2017, and the morning light is beginning to filter in through the cracks of our rugged yurt nestled high up on the Dragon Ridge in the upper Ojai

Valley. I've come for a retreat at the Ojai Foundation where
I have taught experiential education for more than twenty
years. I am being joined here by my fellow teachers, healers,
and facilitators from all over the world, who offer a circle
way called Council: a dialogical practice for adults and children which supports self-reflection and discovery, deepening our relationships, conflict resolution, decision-making,
covisioning, and storytelling. I am looking up through the
skylight, and I see the ice-blue pale hue of dawn's prelude
and a single fading star. Gray limbs of the old oak tree curl
around the circular window frame to embrace the vision.

I lie still, holding on to what I can from the dream the
night before. I wake my friend who lies near me, and we
rise and stretch out of our down sleeping bags into the
chilly air, with frosty breath and sleepy eyes. We slip into
our Uggs while still in our flannels and grab our blankets
and pillows. As we open the old creaking wooden door
and step into the light, we hear the crows calling. *Come*,
they say. We do. Everything here in the mountains of Ojai
is an act of listening, of observing, of being in existence
without premeditation or forethought.

We ascend the hillside, where we look over the blanket
of fog as it recedes into the valley below. The morning dew
is dripping from the branches. We tiptoe into the beautiful circular, wooden-domed Council house, where others
waking from their yurts begin to gather. The room is held
in by large glass doors, and the arched windows bring a
pure rose light of dawn into the space.

We all lie down on pillows in a circle, face up in our
cozy blankets, heads together in the center. We are here

for a Dreamstar, a weaving of stories from the shared liminal space between sleeping and waking, a place where we travel together in an imaginal field. The room is still warm from the singing and dancing the night before. Our guide sits on the outside of our circle and invites us into stillness with a deep sonorous strike of the black Ching bowl. I close my eyes and breathe into the vaulted wooden ceiling as I cross the threshold into dreamtime—perhaps a dream from the past, or a reverie in that very moment, or an instance of prescience that may be revealed later as I listen to others.

I float in the field of the room, feel-sensing when to share my vision out loud with my peers, just as they are doing the same. One by one, we speak our stories, always in the voice of present time, listening for when to be silent or when to give voice to the room: attunement. In this space, intuition does not belong to any one person. It belongs to us all, and we are all here in the field together. We cannot see each other's faces, but we can feel each other's heat and stirring. As each voice speaks its turn, I wonder, *Whose voice is that?... Their story sounds so much like mine.*

I wait until I feel a stirring, then I speak.

How do I describe my intuition? As a child, I possessed an inner knowing, and I do not wonder but think that this is just how we all are wired. On a deep level, I understand these are not coincidences. They are readings from our natural collective inner voice. As children, we are closer to our intuition but may not know its name, like the time as a tiny tot I am sleeping next to my great aunt Jeannette and hear a scurrying on the ceiling above us in the dark. I feel a cold sense in my belly, a knowing. "Scorpion," I cry out. Aunt Jeannette jumps up and turns on the light, and sure enough, there it is, a big one, coming down the wall toward the bed. Or in 1955 when my distressed mother's voice rang out in another room while on the telephone, "Oh no, Sally, that's awful!" Before she could even tell me, I already know. *Polio*. I am right. Joannie, my childhood friend, has contracted polio.

I listened to that voice again and again as I grew older, and though I did not know at the time, the deep listening I had experienced for many years propelled me into a life-altering event one night in 1974. Overcoming fear, I embraced fate and the field.

It's a cold winter night in the Eastern High Sierra. The stars are ablaze, and the Milky Way stretches from pole to pole. I am a passenger with my friend, Little John, in his notorious VW Bug. The engine merrily buzzes along California's Highway 395 as he drops it into high gear, and we scream with delight. I am happy to be back with Johnny, my lifelong friend, who I have spent summers with as a teenage girl, together terrorizing the mountains and valleys of Mono County.

I look southwest across the snow-covered sagebrush flats, up toward Parker Lake and the Mt. Wood bench. I see a fire where no fire should be, an orange blaze emanating through the trees high up on the mountainside. I point it out to Johnny, and we pull off the road to check it out. A strange place for a campfire, it's about a mile to the base of the mountain and perhaps another half mile up. I feel a cold, smooth stone in the pit of my gut, weighing down inside me. Is it fear, or is it fate? *This isn't just any blaze, it's a beacon*, the stone in my gut tells me. *Something's different. Something doesn't feel right.* Johnny and I lock eyes. We have to go up there and find out.

Johnny is the driver for the town school bus and is used to driving big equipment through any kind of mountain weather, so when he takes off full speed, I know we're in good hands. He spins off the highway at the next road as we race toward the blaze. We come to a fork in the road. "Which way?" he shouts. The stone inside me rocks, aiming itself toward a direction. "That way," I say, as I point left. We careen up to the base of the mountain as the road veers south. He cautiously begins approaching the climb in front of us, putting the VW into low gear. We begin the ascent, climbing higher and higher, with the wheels slipping and sliding over the rough, snowy terrain. The Bug starts to drift, and we lose traction. Johnny backs all the way down the road to get a running start, hell-bent on reaching our goal, wheels slipping, snow, mud, and rocks flying as we aim steeper up the mountain.

Through the tall pine trees up ahead, rays of strange light appear, dancing and bobbing erratically through the branches—something different than a fire's glow. We are about to crest the hill when suddenly a huge vehicle with blinding headlights lurches through the trees, barreling down on us. But for some reason, it doesn't stop. It continues toward us with no braking in sight. Johnny slams the VW into reverse, trying to back down the hill as the truck grows nearer. On our left, a massive cliff, too steep to veer down. On our right, boulders the size of brownstones. Suddenly the truck veers into an outcropping of piñon pines and comes to a sudden stop, its nose peeking over the edge of the cliff. All is silent, save for the rumbling of the engines.

"Stay in the car," Johnny whispers.

My heart is in my throat, adrenaline pumping. Johnny grabs a big Maglite and cautiously approaches the cab of the two-ton forestry vehicle. Inside, Johnny finds the driver, slumped over the steering wheel and semiconscious. Johnny signals me to stay put. The man looks up to Johnny, his burned and bloody face smashed in, his wire-rimmed glasses embedded into the bridge of his nose and one of his eyes. He tells Johnny that he works for the US Forest Service, and earlier that day, he was tending to a forestry-ordered slash-and-burn pile. The forestry conducts these slash-and-burns in the winter, making huge piles of deadwood out in open fields, surrounded by snow so that they don't set the rest of the woods on fire. A blazing timber had rolled off the top of one of the fires and smashed the man in the face. Johnny immediately goes into triage. He sloshes back down to me in the ruts of the snow and ice. He is breathing heavily and tells me that the driver of the truck is severely wounded and that I will have to back the Bug down the hill so he can drive the wounded forester to the emergency center in town.

I am scared but confident as I drive backward down the dangerous, precipitous hill, in the night, in the dark, in the snow and ice, ten miles from civilization. I am afraid, but I tell myself I will make it. The wheels slip and slide backward underneath me until I can pull over at the bottom of the grade so Johnny can pass. The sleet and snow flies off the back wheels as I follow the lumber truck back into town to the small emergency facility. Feeling urgency and hope at the same time, I breathe easier now, the weight inside lifting.

We could have just ignored the blaze as we drove down that highway, shrugged it off. If I had shown hesitation or fear and not listened to the cry for help I was feeling from the field, Johnny and I would not have gone on that wild adventure and possibly saved that forester's life.

With life's hurried pace, I have frequently not listened to that voice. In those moments, I am disconnected from the origins of my nature—listening, watching, feeling—what we now call *mindfulness*. We have a natural interior rhythm that can connect with the larger collective consciousness, if we choose to use it. Thinking more with our instinctive center, our hearts, rather than our brains, we can receive the natural information we need. When I fret and think too much with my brain instead of my body—when I don't slow down to attune—that's when bad things can happen.

It's 2005. My husband, Russ, has received several beautiful, illuminated awards from the county and city of Los Angeles for his work as a celebrated actor in film and as a native of the city. I am in the never-ending process of shifting things around to organize what I call *like with like*, which means putting all things alike together in one place. I am in our old 1920s garage that serves as an art studio and storage for all of our family memorabilia. There is a sturdy filing cabinet with drawers that slide as slick as ice. *Is this a good place to put them?* I ask myself.

Will I listen to the answer, or will I ignore it?

The awards are in beautiful portfolio binders and are too large to fit inside the cabinet; I'll just put them on top instead. I look up at the stucco ceiling just above the cabinet. Strange. (Why did I look up?) Water stains are on the ceiling. I hesitate. The stone anchors inside me. *We've used this space for thirty years, and it's never leaked,* I convince myself. *These are just old stains from long ago. Besides, the landlord just put a new surface on the deck above us.* Furthermore, I am too busy to listen to my fears. Satisfied, I put the awards on top of the cabinet and leave.

I return a few days later to find all the memorabilia soaked. The apartment upstairs had a leak under the sink, and as water will do, it found its way into the exact spot I had scoped out. The folders are soggy and the precious certificates blurred around the edges.

I shake my head and scold myself, *I told you, I told you! When will you listen?*

In 2012, I'm preparing to meet my daughter Amber in Virginia for a show where we are performing music and poetry together, after which I'll head to San Francisco to celebrate the release of my album with my record label, Light Rail Records. I'm in a mad flurry of preparation, checking off a list of everything I need to bring. My guitar for the shows, check. Set list, check. Boarding pass and travel information, check. My special magic boots I wear for performances, check. I rush to the laundry room to finish the last bits of laundry and notice a sign on the telephone pole outside.

*Guard Your Possessions*
*Many Recent Burglaries In This Neighborhood*

I tell Russ about the sign, and he says, "Maybe you should put your family heirlooms in our hiding place," a secret compartment he built in our house. I figure the locked drawer in our bedroom is good enough—burglaries usually only happen when opportunities present themselves.

*Are you sure?* The stone inside me heaves. I'm sure.

I move on, but the warning signs keep coming. I accidentally leave my magic boots at the hotel in Virginia, and they are never found. Other things disappear. By the time I get to San Francisco, where I meet up with Russ, we wake to an earthquake and then a phone call from our neighbor. Someone has broken into our apartment through a window on the alley side of the building—poor Russ forgot to lock it. The bad news comes tumbling out of the phone as Russ and I ask our neighbor to check for the jewelry: it's gone. The locked box is battered and broken open. Five generations, one-hundred-and-fifty-years' worth of precious family history is removed from my life and my grandchildren's future, forever. We leave San Francisco and head home, no celebration of my album, only devastation.

*What is it going to take,* I ask myself, *for me to learn how to listen, from the outside in?*

The robbers are eventually found by a detective using fingerprints obtained from the windowsill where they entered. Just some dumb kids doing petty crime, with no clue as to the significance of what they've stolen from my family. At one of the kid's homes, a piece of jewelry is identified as mine: a small black ebony cross outlined in gold that belonged to my great-great-grandmother Alice, the wife of Colonel John Jay Young, my great-great-grandfather who fought on the side of the Union in the Civil War. She would hold that cross and pray for his safe return every day, and one day he finally did come home.

In 1980, when my mother was on her deathbed, throwing her last punch in a long, brutal fight against ovarian cancer, I placed that cross in her hand and prayed so hard for her ancestors to come bring her home. As if she knew the cross was there, her frail fingers closed to hold it, and she let go of her life in the same moment.

It is the only piece of the stolen heirlooms that is rescued that day from the thief's house, and it just so happens to be one of the most valuable to me, personally. I am stunned when the detective has me identify it—I am speechless, suddenly overjoyed, still in my deep sadness. Why was this one piece the only one that was returned to me and not any of the others? It is an affirmation that the ancestors are also in the field, that what once was still is, that every heartbreaking experience holds a lesson about listening to our intuition, if we will allow ourselves to.

★ ★ ★

Another memory of the Upper Ojai Valley comes to me. It's 2015 and the morning after a monstrous storm. I'm on the land facilitating Council with high school seniors for a Senior Rites of Passage retreat, a tradition for teenagers to transition into another chapter and year of their lives. Right now, they are wandering in the wilderness, enjoying the gifts of nature as their teacher. Most of these students have been in the practice of Council throughout their school years, a practice where we sit in a circle facing one another and listen and speak from our hearts without fear of judgment or opinion. Opinion and judgment are merely stories that have lost their narrative. Perhaps you remember a time set aside in kindergarten where you had show-and-tell in a circle on the floor, each child having the opportunity to share as the others are invited to listen. Simply, when it is your turn to speak, we listen to you—something five-year-olds can often do better than grown-ups! We gain wisdom from the gifts of many and connect to the Voice of the Circle, the one that speaks for us all. Learning these tools has brought me into authenticity with all beings. It's a generous way to live, to listen deeply without the interjection of our thoughts, without planning what you are going to say, and then to speak from that place of intuition, in that moment.

The sun is starting to set. The students have had their time with nature. The bell is rung, and it beckons the students back to the beautiful Council house to take their seats in circle. There is one student who we will call Coyote

because of his wandering curiosity and divergent partici-
pation. We wait and wait, and he is late. The land is particularly rugged and dangerous today because of the heavy
rains the night before. The group leader says we will wait
till he gets here.

*No*, the voice inside me speaks. *Go find him.* This time,
I listen and follow.

I excuse myself, not to draw attention, and I leave. I am
walking down the path, past the entrance archway by an
old toyon tree burned by a fire from years ago. It is black
and gnarled, with a large heavy limb arched close to the
path. With no particular sense of direction, I wander until
I find Coyote coming up the road ahead. I signal to him
to hurry, and he quickens his pace. He apologizes; he did
not hear the bell. I give a loving admonishment that it is
all in good time. We pass back under the toyon tree, and I
tell him the story of the fire that swept through this land
years ago. We stand and take note, honor the blackened
limbs that were allowed to remain. Then we return to the
Council house and take our seats.

Shortly after, the land steward comes into the room with
a warning: she tells us the massive toyon tree has collapsed,
its heavy trunk shattering across the path where the student
and I had just been walking. She says to avoid that area, to
choose another way out.

*Ding.* The bell rings again, the warning is received but
so is the lesson.

When I don't listen to my intuition, to the field, the outcome reflects a silencing of myself, a conclusion I very likely
could have helped alter, had I followed through, like Russ's

memorabilia on the cabinet, my family heirlooms. But when I *do* listen to that voice inside me, that pulling stone in my gut which tells me to heed caution or take action—the scorpion climbing down the wall, the High Sierra mountain with Little John, Coyote under the toyon tree—I am almost never steered wrong. And if there is mystery in the telling of these stories, children, that is because much of how intuition reveals itself is exactly like that: just when we are not looking for it, there it is, revealed in the listening, in the quiet space between.

Back to the beginning of the story, to the Dreamstar in 2017, in the Council house, our heads together in the circle.

We share our reveries and visions for a good while until there is silence and a feeling of completion. The sun crests the hill to spill golden warmth into the room. Our guide once again rings the black Ching bowl. He invites us to speak into the center and to witness what we have heard from each other during this collective dreamtime. Then, still on our backs, we weave out loud and we witness back to one another the vivid phrases and words we have heard spoken in the room. The spirit of our stories, commonalities, landscapes, colors, rhythms, and the patterns of our human existence—from the deepest listening—spirals round our center. The room is full of sun now, and we turn over to face one another, beaming brightly, seeing our eyes full of wonder for the first time.

We are all deeply interwoven, to each other, and to ourselves. All we have to do is hear what was always there, always guiding us from within.

*pillows in a circle    he drops it into high    the fog recedes.*

*in the pit of my gut   magic boots  a smooth, heavy stone inside me  slumped over the wheel.*

*go left, that way    I see a fire where no fire should be    sense of place, self and other.*

*Is this a good place to put them    Is it fear or is it fate    Earthquake*

*One-hundred-and-fifty-years            never steered wrong.*

*a loving admonishment    forethought    I am scared but confident*

*I convince myself        small ebony cross        let go*

*what is it going to take        the voice of the circle.*

*without premeditation or present time.*

*do we follow.*

*notice a sign.*

*choose another way out.*

*listen.*

# A Brief Cartography of My Hands

By Lidia Yuknavitch
Author

*My Love Affair with Rocks, Sticks, and Dirt*

Alone is a real place.

Alone might be the most real place I've ever fully em-bodied. Alone is where I am when I conjure characters, where I create storytelling and where I let go the world of so-called authorities telling me to be something or do something else. Alone is how I learned the power of the invented story to combat the lies aimed to keep me small, quiet, and well-behaved. It's where I can hear voices and trust them, where I can taste salt and hear the secrets of trees. Alone, as it turns out, has been everything.

Alone was first a vacant lot across the street from my childhood home. The words *vacant lot* just mean a piece of land that is not being used, you know, a place between things where kids play or animals and plants do whatever they want. Except that my mother was a real estate agent, so *vacant lot* also meant a piece of property that could yet be assigned a value, sold, and bought, which I understood at a fairly young age. Sometimes I had to go to open houses with her. I wondered for years when the vacant lot would shift from a liminal space to a construction site or some new homes in our cul-de-sac. My home was a vacant heart, which is why *alone* took on such vital meaning to me. It gave me the courage to risk trusting my intuition and hone in on my formidable story-making abilities. Meanings live underneath the surface of things.

My very first best friends were not people. Dirt, sticks, rocks, leaves, the bark of madrones and Douglas fir trees. Dirt in particular mesmerized me. I buried so many things in the dirt in that vacant lot. Rocks, pennies, pieces of paper on which I'd drawn a sun, a tree, or a boat on some ocean, a spoon, a pair of underwear, a metal toy jeep, and several of my father's architectural drawing pens. Very fancy pens, not regular pens. They were to me, anyway, as a child impossibly obsessed with objects. Faber-Castell pens.

I also used to eat dirt, small stones, paper, and bark, sometimes while hiding out in the vacant lot, dreaming up worlds where being a kid and being a tree or earth or a rock could somehow merge. The Pacific Northwest rain growing us.

The day I buried the Faber-Castell pens in the ground, my father called me into the kitchen after dinner, where he leaned against the sink he'd never washed a dish in, in kind of a casual, architect pose, his arms crossed a little beautifully across his chest. As usual, I had no idea where my mother was, in some other vacancy, some liminal space.

"Let me see your hands," he said.

One time I took his fancy pens and drew imagined maps on both of my palms and arms. So he already knew I had an interest in his pens. Repeat offender. To me, the pens were magical objects, and I was a child who secreted away magical objects.

When you are a child who lies and hides and eats dirt as a means of survival, you know immediately in your chest how to turn to your own imagination to get by. When his anger grew big as a house, when my fear threatened to eat me alive, when my shame reddened my face and made the top of my head so hot I thought I was on fire, I invented an exit strategy. How to sprout branches for arms, shoots coming from my heart and ribs. How to make my mouth a stone ready to hurl.

When he asked me why my hands were covered in dirt, when he asked me if I knew where his Faber-Castell pens were, I let my mind go and let the tree that was me take over. I did what I knew how to do.

I lied.

"I don't know." I looked down at the shitty gray linoleum of our kitchen floor. I stole a glance at the wood of the cabinets. I wondered if they still had tree memories. One thing I did not do was consider telling him the truth. *I buried your fancy pens in the vacant lot like they were people— a father, a mother, a child. Under a madrone tree. I placed the deep green waxen leaves over each mound like perfect grave blankets.* "Maybe someone broke into our house." I cast worried eyes in the direction of a window. I pictured robbers entering our house, taking only his pens. I pictured myself with binoculars watching the house from the vacant lot. Like a kid spy. I don't know why. I only know when I lied to him, my hands, spine, and ribs began to vibrate.

*Lidia, where are my pens, goddamn it?*

*I don't know.*

It wasn't my first lie.

It wasn't my worst lie.

It wasn't even a very interesting lie, to be honest. So why even tell you about it at all? Because it was around this time that my hands began to speak to me. And anyway, the worst things that have happened to me are not always where the story is hiding, a truth it's taken me a very long time to understand.

When I say my hands began to speak to me, I mean that weird vibrating feeling that I had when I lied was real to me. I mean my imagination was moving toward form. I began to fill notebooks with drawings and words, stories that had nothing to do with this family, this house, this vacant-hearted place. Taking his pens was an act of rebellion, resistance, resilience. Stealing them required stealth and strength. My lie in the face of his rage was the first seed of a kind of full-body truth coming, my intuition getting born: *Take the pens. Bury the pens. When his rage comes, even as a fist, trust that your story is bigger than the blow. And he can't touch your storytelling. It lives in the dirt in a vacant lot next to trees much taller and older than he will ever be.*

He yelled at me for a while. I stared hard at the wood of our kitchen cabinets while he bellowed above me.

The fancy fucking pens had worth because they were his.

"Your daughter is a liar, Dorothy." His voice crescendoed through to the living room at the end of his shame speech.

I mean, he couldn't actually *prove* I'd stolen his pens. "A goddamn little liar. Now, finish washing those dishes." As if that was something I inherited from her. Lying, I mean. Or washing dishes. I guess we'd both temporarily forgotten she was out with clients at a closing, dealing with earnest monies and transfers of property, home ownership.

The word *Dorothy* sort of hung in the kitchen air there for a bit, emptied out of meaning…except secretly I thought about *The Wizard of Oz*, and the dishwater was warm and soapy around my submerged hands, and what a superhuman power it must be to create whole worlds of story where animals and trees and poppies and emerald cities and twisters brought hue and song and girls to life. It's a good secret that people who wash dishes keep. That we are inside a liminal space, there with our hands submerged in water, touching something from before we were born. I washed the dirt off my hands while I cleaned each dish. I stared at my hands in the dishwater. Palms up.

When I look back at myself as an image and story, my hands look like little psalms, little songs of becoming, the hands of a daughter thief, the hands of a girl who drew too much, the hands of a girl who was making stories before she knew what to do with them.

*On Lying*
Lying to survive is different than lying inside some kind of religious matrix of sin and redemption or weird cults of morality and good citizenship. When you lie to survive, when telling the truth is the danger that puts your body or your dreams of getting out or your life at stake—and there

are legions of children whose lives are at stake for thousands of different reasons—lying is an act of intense intuition. You have to turn away from everything you've been told. You have to believe in your own version of yourself without logic or conscious reasoning. You can't think your way out. You have to feel into a fiction and believe in the possibility of transport.

I'm saying that now, looking back at myself as a kid, playing alone in the dirt underneath the fir trees and madrones. I'm not looking back at that kid wondering what's wrong with her. Tsk tsk, too bad her moral compass went awry so early. Why is she lying? And I'm not thinking she's going to hell, that one, like my father's sister told me I would. I think that's an idiotic line of thought, actually; idiotic questions to ask of children whose imaginations are just getting born. I know why some kids lie. Some kids are trying to story their way out of a bigger lie called *family* or *father* or *mother* or *home* or *society*. Some kids are reaching for an identity.

So from where I sit now, I'm saying *Fuck yeah* to that kid me in the past, whose little lies about pens of course bloomed into bigger lies (the art of storying can take what breaks you and give it form) and those bigger lies into whole chapters of life, relationships, epic failures and mistakes, lying her way out, charting her way into the unknown, not just rejecting the logics around her meant to pin her down but openly defying them. One story at a time.

I collect vintage writing pens. A Sheaffer Imperial. A red Parker Duofold. A Waterman's 52. An Esterbrook J. Three Conway Stewart 388s. The casings decorated in deep greens, marble reds, intricate browns, with design casings like the bark of magnificent trees. I used to handwrite everything with one of these magical pens, until the day my hands hurt too much to write by hand.

I have buried a pen underneath a tree everywhere I have ever lived.

Some of us put our hands into dirt rather than lifting them toward higher order, a father, *Our Father*, patriarchal forms forced upon the bodies of children, just some words infinitely less interesting to a kid than a vacant lot. Some of us come early to the idea that imagination is a real place, a place capable of rivaling the material conditions of struggle and pain. There is a path from imagination to intuition open to anyone willing to step away from other stories meant to keep us from becoming our full and best selves.

Which is another way of saying when your intuition shows up, listen up: it just might be a story getting born. And storytelling can save your life. Storytelling is an intuitive artistic practice, a form of resistance, revolution.

*Imaginary Friends*

My intuition took on her best forms inside uneasy situations where what was in front of me was a far worse lie than anything coming from inside my body. But I needed to talk to someone about this alternate reality—badly— and thus my imagination bloomed with a vengeance from rocks and sticks and dirt to imaginary friends. I know so very many writers and artists who had imaginary friends as kids, particularly those who came from troubled homes. Maybe it's a prerequisite. The names I gave my two imaginary friends were Boca and Modart. They were better than sticks. When my older sister learned Spanish she filled the house with a beautiful new-to-me language, so that's where

Boca came from. I have no idea where Modart came from, though I have a theory. I think I may have misheard the name Mozart. Or else it shifted in my mouth and mind when I took piano lessons.

By the age of ten, I had successfully created an elaborate internal realm, almost as if I moved the vacant lot with its trees and shrubs and animals into my body. I didn't just *think* this world with Boca and Modart and a turtle and birds and trees like sentries was true and real. I *trusted* the reality. Modart in particular once told me to imagine my own rib cage as if the ribs were branches on a great tree that lived in my chest, my arms and hands like branches and leaves. Fairly quickly after conjuring up Boca and Modart, I recognized that they could help me through my external reality. Soon, I was hallucinating—inducing a dream state either involuntarily or with some kind of kid power—at every moment of crisis. *Be a tree. Be a tree. Be a tree that lives in the vacant lot.*

Trusting my intuition, born of my imaginal world, transported me beyond crisis.

My entire childhood was a never-ending series of staccato crises.[10]

---

10   For clarity, and with respect to children and adults who suffer from auditory or visual hallucinations, I did indeed experience such hallucinations as a child, a fact that, when I finally told her, sent my mother into a panic that her child might be insane, in addition to having the condition pica, an eating disorder in which a person eats things not usually considered food. For a short period of time I was prescribed lithium for the voices and iron for the pica. The more I was out of the house away from my father at swim practice, the more my conditions improved. Periodically as an adult the conditions return, usually during times of high stress, pain, or crisis; for example, when my daughter died, or when my mother was dying, or when my son was born. Becoming a writer has given me a real place to express what feels internally impossible on an external plane where, mercifully, beautiful forms might emerge. Self-destruction dissipates in favor of self-expression.

The imagination of a child is formidable.

I was learning to stay alive by imagining tree me. Tree me? Tree me had seasons, and each season brought different stories up from the good dirt to my feet roots up into my gut and out to my branches, spreading like wild starshoot into my hands.

## Alone

Alone to me now is being inside art-making. A fully embodied realm where inside and outside speak easily to one another, having left their binary positions to play. I have learned to trust my conscious and subconscious interplay. I have learned how to let voices become characters. I have learned to put my hands to their best use, drawing, painting, telling stories, planting flowers and vegetables, petting the head of the dog or the belly of a cat, soothing someone back to sleep in the night, my hand on their back.

The first seed of any story for me begins inside an image or a feeling or a phrase that is not logical, a place of nonsense, a place of pure imaginal energy (remember the vacant lot—that liminal space where anything could become). I let that image or feeling or phrase come through my body into my hands. It helps to close your eyes, actually, while writing or typing, even if it makes a mess (remember digging in dirt, even eating dirt). The image or feeling or phrase has to come to life for me so that I can follow it, and in order to follow it, I have to believe with my whole body that not knowing where the story is going is still a real place to be (remember how inventing stories saved your life). If the first impulse of a story idea vibrates my spine and hands and ribs, I know to keep going. If I can't tell what will happen next, I know to trust the thrill of creating. If the story emerging in front of me is impossible, I know to double down (remember what they are telling you is a lie to keep you small and quiet and afraid).

A story my mother loved to tell when she was still alive was about the day she came driving home in her station wagon from a real estate closing and caught a glimpse of me high up in a tree in the vacant lot. She stopped the car. She rolled down her window. She looked up at me; I looked down at her. I remember she looked small. "I never knew how she got up so high in that tree," she'd say, telling the story with her Southern drawl. "She was wearing a long floral-printed dress. I wasn't sure she would come down." I don't know exactly why my mother loved to tell this story. Sometimes I look at photos of her and wonder. Maybe it impressed her to see her daughter at such a great height. Maybe she caught a glimpse of my will. Or maybe she remembered something about herself as a girl. My mother never went to college, but she was a born storyteller.

*Here Is a Map*
Listen, here is a limitation of mine that is very important. I cannot write a word unless there are trees and water present. The water needn't be next to me, although that helps. As long as I can get to the water periodically, I can restore my imaginal core by staring at the ocean or the river or just standing in rain. Of water I have written whole oceans. The trees need to be quite near. Near enough to speak to them.

If you live in a place in your life that eats away your soul from your body, get out. You already know what nourishes you. You do. You already know how to create the world you need around you in order to story yourself back to life. It isn't some magical pen. The pen isn't where the worth lives. The worth is you.

You are worth everything. You always were.

It's in your hands.

# Mystic Lessons

By Jia Tolentino
*Writer*

In the summer of 2019, I flew to France with my friend Emma for a trip bookended by my waking up with an *infection urinaire* on our first morning and having a wasp sting me inside my open mouth on the last night. The week between, though, was a sweet and lazy river—a stained-glass honeyed-sunlight fields-and-castles reverie. We drove aimlessly around Normandy, reading out loud from poorly translated guidebooks. One night, under a silvery twilight that was reflected in the slowly rising water around our paved walkway, we carried our bags to Mont-Saint-Michel, the surreal tidal island and former medieval monastery. There was just one tiny inn within the island itself, and so it fell silent once the sky darkened and the throngs of people flooded out. We wandered, stoned and quiet, through chapels and gardens. I was transfixed by a graveyard where the cold monuments seemed to cry and flower and reach for the sky.

Emma and I had been talking about what it might have been like to live in a monastery. I had been thinking about the ahistorical gift of self-determination, of being a woman who had spent much of her twenties writing all day and all night. In a place like Mont-Saint-Michel, where the stones themselves seemed held together by history, it felt especially tangible that—despite my well-practiced complaints about the various immoral and destructive aspects of contemporary living—my entire existence was an unlikely luxury. If I were to disappear and reappear at a random place on the fabric of planetary space-time, I had a high chance of materializing as a subsistence farmer in an era before antibiotics: a woman married off mid-puberty, with no books in the house, no access to solitude, and little in the way of sexual or reproductive choice.

We went back to the inn and sat on the balcony, looking at the walkway snaking out into the dark. On the mountain, you could see anything coming from miles away. You could prepare a loving welcome. You could mount a defense. That summer, I was on the precipice of switching my psychological orientation toward pregnancy from aversion to desire—I had been walking slowly, for years, toward a door I would soon knock on in the dark.

I was in gentle, preemptive mourning for my life of impulsivity and consciously wielded independence. In that moment, wearing the black night like a blanket, I felt a new understanding of what religious consecration meant for women in bygone centuries: it was a way—perhaps the only sanctioned way—to receive freedom from pregnancy, labor, and childrearing. It was a way to never live in service of babies or of men. I had nursed an obsession with medieval female mystics for years, admiring them primarily as writers. But I saw then that I loved them—Julian of Norwich, Hildegard of Bingen, Catherine of Siena, Clare of Assisi, Margery Kempe, and others—for finding a way to do, so many years ago, what so many women in our era of deceptive bounty still dream of. They had built unbreachable stone walls around the things that were most precious to them: their faith, yes, but also their time, their minds, their intuition.

The scholar Monica Furlong writes that, for a medieval woman, life generally "began with a limited, often purely domestic, education, followed by marriage in the mid-teens or earlier...the marriage would be followed by repeated pregnancies and the births of many children." Childbirth, back then, was an event that wore a strong association with death. Furlong cites Catherine of Siena, the fourteenth-century Italian mystic, as an example: Catherine was the twenty-fourth of twenty-five children, half of whom had died by the time she was born. Catherine was one of premature twins when she was born in 1347. By this point, half of her twenty-two other siblings had already died; soon afterwards, Catherine's twin died too.

She was fifteen when her sister Bonaventura died during labor and the duty to marry Bonaventura's widower summarily fell to her. But Catherine refused, cutting off her hair and going on a hunger strike. As she later told her friend and mentor Raymond of Capua, she built a cell in her own mind from which she could not flee. She began living as a recluse in her family's home and then turned, radically, toward a life of outward-facing public service: she became a preacher and a reformer, rejecting the other roles that were available to her, finding a choice beyond living as a mother or a nun.

When Catherine was around thirty—three years before she would die, weakened by a lifetime of extreme fasting—she entered an ecstatic state of communion with God. The theology that emerged was simple and psychedelic: God was life itself—a sea in which we were all fish. "Every step of the way to heaven is heaven," she wrote.

A few female mystics had to carve out a path within the bounds of marriage. Margery Kempe, the author of the first autobiography in English, had over a dozen children with her husband before convincing him to swear to mutual celibacy. Her mystical conversion began after the birth of her first child in the late 1390s, which prompted months of terrifying hallucinations. It was solidified in 1413, when she visited an elderly Julian of Norwich, who assured Kempe that her visions of God were real.

Julian was an anchoress—she had taken a vow, as a young adult, to permanently enclose herself in a doorless cell attached to a church. When anchorites were enclosed, they would receive the sacrament of the dying; when they died, the windows in their cells would simply be sealed. In exchange for this, they received a profound and formal religious authority—in church hierarchy, none were above them except the bishop. Most anchorites were anchoresses;

in the thirteenth century, women in anchor-holds out-
numbered men four to one.

Julian was born in the middle of the fourteenth century in England and witnessed the Black Death as a young
child. Little is known about her otherwise—even her last
name is lost to history—and she is the mystic I have always
loved most. The force of her theological vision is thunder-
ous and overwhelming, a fullness more remarkable given
the absolute attenuation of her surroundings: you picture
the meals slipped in through the window, the solitary pac-
ing, the entire world compressed to four walls.

Her great revelations occurred when she was around
thirty, when a bout of sickness brought her close to death.
For Julian and many other female mystics, Furlong writes,
"the cost of becoming visible and audible, of taking a path
with no role model walking ahead, was considerable, and
the women paid for it." The knowledge that they sought was
the type of knowledge that can only come through being
alone, through allowing themselves to be shattered: this was
the path, after all, that Jesus himself had taken to the cross.

Like Catherine, many of the female mystics practiced severe asceticism. Clare of Assisi, born in Italy at the end of
the twelfth century, governed her order of nuns, the Poor
Clares, with an extreme vow of poverty that doubled as an
assertion of equality. As the scholar Elizabeth Alvilda Petroff
writes, Clare believed that "she and her sisters could support themselves, as Christ's followers did in the gospels, by

the work of their hands and by begging alms; she did not believe that women had to be supported economically by others, and she did not want to own property and live off its income." To demonstrate that women needed no special coddling, the Poor Clares went barefoot in winter and slept on the ground. "The physical austerities undergone by women mystics, and that young women often imposed on themselves, underscored society's need to control and purify the female body," Petroff writes. "But in the case of women who were put away in the religious life, something unexpected happened. The very techniques of prayer and meditation that were supposed to reinforce the withdrawal of a religious woman, to 'contain and suppress' the body, turned into a powerful force that made women potent visionaries."

These mystics are one of my last strands of connection to the religion I grew up with—these women, and their irradiating desire to search for something beyond the visible, some access to a kaleidoscoping realm of presence and love and terror. That desire has filtered through to me, though I've followed it in such ordinary contexts, seeking out bouts of extreme solitude and overwhelming physical experience, in the midst of what is an otherwise profoundly conventional life. I feel stunned by the lack of compromise in the lives of these mystics, the clarity of their intuition. Particularly in this respect: they repudiated motherhood personally but valorized it theologically. They "manipulated the dominant tradition to free themselves from the burdens of fertility yet made female fertility a powerful symbol," the scholar Caroline Walker Bynum writes. They conceived of Christ's body in female terms: it bled, it gave new life through its blood, it transfigured itself into food. After all, God had made the womb the foundation of his essential salvific miracle; after all, Jesus's most divine act is profoundly analogous to a mother's labor. "For when the hour of your delivery came," the thirteenth-century mystic Marguerite of d'Oingt wrote, "you were placed on the hard bed of the cross…your nerves and all your veins were broken." Julian wrote down a vision of God expressing the kind of sacrificial love that is knit into a mother before she ever meets her child, as the agony of pregnancy and childbirth is subsumed into hope that her creation will be safe, will be saved. "If I could suffer more," Julian heard God saying, "I would suffer more."

Six months after that trip to France, I got pregnant, and then two months later, the pandemic took hold. My boyfriend and I relocated to Upstate New York, to the house we'd bought after I sold my book. I had formerly associated solitude with stretches of psychedelic loneliness or furious writing; I had always craved isolation as the equivalent of a dark room, a sort of temporary anchor-hold, in which my thoughts would flare like lighted matches. But there was nothing like that in pandemic isolation: no sparks, no sharpness. Isolation in the woods, with trees and space and sunlight—this was another instance of ahistorical, arbitrary, undeserved luck. As my body expanded, I felt like a slowly growing plant, like a strong and sweet and capacious animal. I stopped writing and felt myself moving toward a different kind of knowledge, one that required not force and sharpness but instead surrender, patience, the willingness to be a vessel for time.

I began to understand that this was part of what the medieval female mystics had intuited. In studying these women, I had always seen—and identified with—primarily a tormenting, salvific, internally generated desire to render thoughts onto paper. Peter Dronke writes that the "medieval woman's motivation for writing at all seems rarely to be predominantly literary: it is often more urgently serious than is common among men writers; it is a response springing from inner needs, more than from an artistic, or didactic, inclination." But their openness to revelation had left them open to the truth about it: that transformative experience is rarely entirely legible right away. When Julian of Norwich first wrote down her visions of God soon after she experienced them, she excluded certain scenes because she knew she didn't yet grasp the nature of what she'd seen. Around fifteen years later, she began to understand what had been revealed to her, and then five years later, in 1393—twenty years after the revelations—she wrote everything down in full.

Was it hard for Julian to wait? From the solitude of her anchor-hold—from within the days that must have sometimes lasted forever—how many times did she try to capture her visions and then fail? Did she trust that labor would lead to epiphany? Hildegard of Bingen, the polymathic twelfth-century German mystic and abbess, described revelation as a sort of transcendent birth: "I saw a mystic and wondrous vision, such that all my womb was convulsed and my body's sensory powers were extinguished, because my knowledge was transmuted into another mode, as if I no longer knew myself." When I was on the hospital bed, I was surprised to find that I had no impatience in me, not one spike of it through twenty-four hours of contractions. I was still timid from the pandemic, maybe—it was months before the vaccines would start to free us—but this was the first time in my life that I knew, absolutely, that revelation would arrive.

I held on to that certainty through the early months with my baby, in the many moments when I felt rage burn through me: I was so depleted, I wanted to be alone again, I wanted silence and a blank page and an unstoppable urge to fill it. But I knew that I wasn't denying myself the tug of my intuition, which had led me over the last decade to fiercely protect my autonomy in a way that made me sure it felt right to—at least temporarily, or intermittently, or partially   give it up.

The mystics had followed their love wherever it led them: to self-effacement, to self-determination, to both intertwined. Clare of Assisi died in 1253, two days after a papal bull certified her rule for her religious community—the first time a woman's rule had ever received approval from the Pope. It's reported that Clare's final words were "Blessed be You, O God, for having created me."

# Crossing Paths with Ghosts: On Creative Process and Reckoning with the History of Women's Intuition

*By Amber Tamblyn*

In the winter of 2009, the actress Brittany Murphy collapsed in her shower and was later pronounced dead at a hospital where doctors tried to revive her. I was sitting at my kitchen table in Venice Beach, California, when I heard the news of her death on the television in the other room. As I looked at her face plastered in memoriam across the TV screen, something shifted in me, as if someone had entered my body and taken a seat inside it.

Brittany and I began our acting careers as child actresses in Los Angeles in the late 80s and early 90s, and like many of the young women who hustled the audition circuit later on in the early aughts, we knew each other from it, from a distance. If you grew up in the limelight of that time, in that particular city, you felt a kinship to other actresses in your peer group who were also navigating that same strange era of Hollywood that felt like one giant in-between; pre– social media influencers but past the point where tabloids were in complete control of your identity. Myspace reigned supreme and a run-in with Lindsay Lohan outside some vodka-sponsored Coach bag party where new pop singer Christina Aguilera performed was inevitable. We were all just one T-Mobile Sidekick screen flip away from a future of personal brands and paying our rent with a single Insta- gram post.

If you were an actress during this time, your body didn't really belong to you. It was commonplace in those days to be asked to lose five pounds for a role, as if that might ac- tually make a difference. Your weight, how you looked, and your sex appeal was a free and open market and as normal to discuss as notes on a script. So while I didn't know Brittany personally, I knew Brittany existentially. I had been her, and she had been me. Undoubtedly, we had both, at one time or another, been in a casting room where our bodies were objectified, or had been trampled by the unique breed of paparazzi that infested those years, or had experienced some abuse at the hands of our industry and by those who upheld its party line.

The last and possibly only time I ever saw Brittany Mur- phy in person was upstairs in casting director Mali Finn's office in Hollywood to read for the role of Alex in Emi- nem's film *8 Mile*. Every actress has their way of entering an audition waiting room: some scan to discreetly see who else is there, some saunter in, while others make jokes and talk to the gay receptionist Kevin for far too long and far too loudly. Most drop their things off and head directly to the bathroom to spend another twenty minutes fixing makeup and running lines in the mirror.

I had my own ritual, which was to signal to others how much I didn't need to be there. I would sign in—my name, the role I was auditioning for, the agency that represented me—then plop down on a couch and put my head down into the pages of the scenes, never once looking up until my name was called. I didn't like talking to anyone else who was there, but many of the actresses, both known and unknown, found community among each other, while sitting on metal fold-up chairs located in cold sterile hallways under fluorescent lighting. Quiet waiting rooms or hallways would turn into vocal social gatherings among young women who bonded over the shared experience of rejections, or the hope and dream of one day making it, of first chances, or, if you were lucky, second ones. They congratulated one another on callbacks or booked jobs, or traded phone numbers to schedule hangouts, or talked shit in low whispers, all while dressed in similar, outlandish costumes for whatever role they were there to audition for: a reformed stripper on the run, a rookie cop with a big secret, the girl with a heart of gold with only two speaking lines but she's Leonardo DiCaprio's love interest (great trade off!) and, of course, Meryl Streep's daughter. Everyone always went in for the role of Meryl Streep's daughter: it was a rite of passage.

I never wanted any part of their community and prided myself on being the Ebenezer Scrooge of an audition waiting room. I was a different breed, I told myself, born and raised in this kooky town, a published poet. Sometimes I would come into a waiting room and go to the sign-in table and write in a fake name, the real part I was auditioning for, and a fake rep just to fuck with whoever was auditioning after me, just to shake things up a little bit. *Gwyneth Paltrow, the part of Alex, repped by Bill Gates.* I acted as if going in for an audition was like stopping by the dry cleaners to pick up a dress I may or may not ever wear again. Taking the piss out of the audition process made me feel safe; it protected me against the eventual rejection I almost always had to hear. By not taking the process before the actual audition seriously, maybe I would be less affected by hearing I didn't get a part I had worked really hard for. But the truth is I was just as nervous as everyone else. I wanted the roles just as badly as everyone else did. I was no better or worse than any of the young women who had also given up their childhoods, their adult lives, and sometimes their dignity for the opportunity.

But as the years went on, I began to feel deeply conflicted about this path I had chosen or, rather, had been chosen for me as a child. My identity had been completely wrapped up in my career as an actress, and my increasing apathy toward the audition process was the first sign that I deeply wanted to get out. I had never before considered what my life would look like if I quit, if I started over on a new path toward some different career. I had been a published poet with two books of poetry out by the time I was twenty-five years old, but that just seemed to some like my hobby. My gut told me I had so much more to offer—so much more to say outside of performing the words that someone else had written.

The door to Mali Finn's office opened, and we all looked up as Brittany Murphy came bounding out of the room, her audition pages in one hand and her purse in the other. She wore all black, with a black skirt and black knee-high boots, and her golden hair bobbed in the air as she headed for the exit. "Amber," said Mali from the casting room's open door, "come on in." In the seconds between Brittany's exit of the room I was about to enter, we crossed paths and locked eyes. She smiled warmly at me, and I was struck by how vibrant and alive her face was. "Good luck," she whispered to me as she passed, and I know she meant it.

Brittany got that role of Alex in *8 Mile*, and five years later I would see her again, in the form of breaking news on my television. She was thirty-two years old.

What I felt that day when Brittany Murphy died—the sense of someone sitting down inside of me—was the activation of my intuition: my creative muscle in full flexion, preparing me for something big that was coming, that had been stirring for a long time. It was an extension, almost a peak, of the gut feeling I had been listening to for years, the one that was resisting auditions and my life as an object to be projected upon. Brittany's life and subsequent death held up a mirror to my life as an actress, but also a startling desire for a death of my own. Not literal, like hers, but existential. Brittany would never go on auditions again, never have to feel the sting of constant rejection, or have her body's weight openly scrutinized, or have to face a casting couch and all that comes with it again. I wanted that same kind of freedom, too. For years, I had been so unhappy on that hamster wheel of competition and wanted more than anything to be seen for the full potential of who I was—who I could become. An actress, yes, but also a film director, a producer, a writer-at-large who wrote screenplays and books. Brittany's death was not personal to me, but it was personal for me. It was an unlikely invitation to the beginning of my ending—that part of me that needed this old way of living to die in order for a new version of myself to be reborn.

What I didn't know then was that that rebirth began the day I saw the news about her death. My intuition was manifesting into a creative conjuring in the form of a new poem I would end up writing in honor and memory of Brittany—a poem that would change the trajectory of my entire life.

On the news, the anchor recounted to viewers how Brittany was found by her mother, crumpled up on the shower floor and unconscious. I was almost instantly struck by the image of a spider just after its death, its many legs closing in on one another like a matted knot of threads. I sat with this image for several days, and each time I returned to it, it flowered, until several more lines began to blossom. "Her body dies like a spider's," the poem began, "In the shower, / The blooming flower / seeds a cemetery. / A pill lodges in the inner pocket of her flesh coat. / Her breasts were the gifts of ghosts. / Dark tarps of success." Once I had those first few lines, I sat down to learn from them, to see what else they wanted to teach me. What was born was the poem "About the Body" (later titled, simply, "Brittany Murphy"), which would go on to be published in *PANK* magazine by literary force Roxane Gay, and which would become one of the many poems in the book *Dark Sparkler* that would take me nearly six more years to write. *Dark Sparkler* was a career-defining work for me, exploring the lives and deaths of child star actresses with the journey of my own existential death included. The book is an inventory of ghosts; an exploration of women as objects, as victims; of fame and the exploited stories of girls in the entertainment industry throughout history. The book is also a reckoning of my life as an actress and my desire to cease, to end—to let die, in a way—the life solely defined by an audition room. *Dark Sparkler* was a huge critical success and sold well, too, and it paved the way for me to be taken seriously as a writer across genres and mediums, as a novelist, essayist, and opinion writer for the *New York Times*.

That feeling of apathy and resistance I had carried in my gut all those years before was leading me toward the writing of that poem, and then that book—toward taking the change I so desperately needed into my own hands. I listened to all the ways in which my intuition guided me toward this freedom and know it is a big part of the reason I have the life I do today, one that exists credibly with worth in both literary and film worlds, as an actress, a director, and a writer.

But back to sitting down at the kitchen table and tapping in. Before my career as a writer, before all the books I wrote, and before Roxane Gay's belief in my work, I had to really pinpoint the way a piece of writing was going to

unfold in me and learn to honor all the feelings that would
bubble up along with it. For many women, this is a physical manifestation which can present in the form of anxiety.
"Extreme visual clarity, tunnel vision, diminished sound,
and the sense that time is slowing down," writes Malcolm
Gladwell in his 2005 book on the adaptive unconscious,
*Blink*. "This is how the human body reacts to extreme
stress." Writing can certainly be an extreme stress: when
I'm deep in the middle of a piece of writing in which I've
hit my stride and maintaining that stride is critical, it requires everything I've got—my whole body and psychic
and intellectual energy firing on all cylinders. I've left long
writing sessions having held my breath on and off for hours,
with numbness and tingling in my arm and neck, with
tunnel vision so fixed on the task at hand, I emerge fully
disoriented as to where I geographically am. My stomach
will tie itself up so tightly I'll lose entire body signals, like
knowing you have to pee or when you're hungry. It can
be a completely out-of-body experience, deeply immersed
in the body.

Connecting your intuition to your creativity and a process that works for you individually, that can be counted
on every time, is much more complicated than just sitting
down to put pen to paper. It requires investigation, experimentation, stamina, and an adjournment of our usual bodily
functions and frames of mind. For me, it always starts with
the sensation that someone else has entered my body and
sat down inside of it, seating themselves squarely in the root
of my guts. I picture a mirror image of myself, an opaque
ghostlike figure double-layered over me, like the scene in

*Annie Hall* when a second Diane Keaton stands up out of herself, only in reverse.

That feeling is usually followed by the whisper of an idea—a few words strung together, a sentence or a line pulled from the air. I carry it with me, sometimes for just a few days or sometimes for months, until it's ready to evolve into something more. This is a sacred time for me as a writer, a time in which I feel a profound responsibility to keep this little thing alive inside of me. Those of us who are mothers can use the same metrics of carrying a baby to term to apply to this different form of incubation. With the sentence now inside me, growing and getting bigger every day, I daydream about its potential, about what I hope it will grow up to be. I give it names, themes, assignments, prompts to help it grow. I play with the notion of what genre it might become, what category it might one day fall into. A poem? A novel? A script? An essay? It will reveal itself eventually, and I can't wait to find out.

When it comes time to give birth—to sit down and write—I always begin to feel that sense of anxiety, that sense of dread or impostor syndrome. Instead of fighting it or getting angry with myself, I let it pass or, rather, let it play out as it needs to. I treat it like a child throwing a much-needed tantrum while I calmly wait nearby. I stare at the blank page in front of me, my mind exploding with doubt, desperate for any distraction to tear me away from it. *You should check Twitter! You should respond back to that email and that thing you don't want to do with a resounding Yes! You should drive an acquaintance you've just met to the airport! You should clean the toilet!* In fact, this initial reaction to distract myself is so strong in me, I'll spend whole weeks doing nothing but meaningless correspondence, reorganizing shelves and closets, unsubscribing from mailing lists, or calling my mom back to help her find her Instagram password for a fifth time. I'll do all this while knowing what I want to write is sitting there in a folder on my desktop, gnawing, picking at me as if I were the scab, just waiting to be opened.

I used to see this as a stalling of my process, but now I see it as a cleansing that's very much a part of my process. I welcome its chaos and let it take whatever time it needs to wear itself out, all the while talking it through its outbursts until we've come out on the other side, together, ready to get to work. *It's okay. You're scared. You think you don't know what you're trying to say, but you know exactly what you need to say. You'll get there, I promise.* Most people can get stuck at this point in their creative journey and see the blank page as a sign of writer's block or a lack of inspiration, and maybe, for some people, it is. For me, this is a period which requires patience and a different perspective: to honor the struggle, the outbursts of the unconscious mind attempting to formulate meaning out of what I'm intuiting. Eventually, whether hours or days later, with a sparkling clean toilet and a calendar full of commitments I will come to regret, all will become very quiet in my head, like being in the eye of a storm. I'll join that someone who has already sat down inside me and take a seat at my desk, my hands lifting toward the keyboard, to begin.

"Intuition and gut feelings are not in opposition to getting information," says psychologist Gerd Gigerenzer, author of

*Gut Feelings: The Intelligence of the Unconscious* in an interview for Econlib. "A gut decision is always one that started out with evidence, and if the evidence doesn't tell you, then you listen to your guts. And listening to your guts only makes sense if you have years of experience [doing it]." The evidence I received that day Brittany's death was announced on the news came in the form of a single opening line: *Her body dies like a spider's.* When evidence of that line did not lead me to an answer in the moment (more lines), I turned to my gut—my intuition as it pertains to my creativity— to explore it further, like an investigation after a murder. *What does the line mean? Where does it want to go? What do I want it to say? What's its intention?* I am able to go through the process of finding this evidence, of listening to my intuition with ease, because I have trained myself to understand how it manifests.

Before this clarity in my process, I went through years of emulating the writing of my mentors, of staring at a blank paper for months in sheer terror while thinking that was stopping me from writing, of following the guidance of famous writers on how to write a book, such as Stephen King's *On Writing.* While King's book is a worthy read, it is still *his* process, not my own. One wouldn't ask Egon Schiele to mix his colors and create a pallet in the same manner as Claude Monet. I needed to learn my own process. To get there, I had to practice; I had to strengthen my intuition.

When I am writing, my intuition is tangible, it is real and something I can identify, but it has taken me years to harvest that strong connection with what one would think should come so easily to me. Women work painstakingly hard to reconnect to their intuitive intelligence because of the many different ways its existence has threatened the patriarchal world throughout history. Gigerenzer says that gut feelings are not arbitrary, they are not a sixth sense, but there is still widespread suspicion around them stemming from age-old oppressions. "Such investigation is inherently controversial," Rupert Sheldrake concurs with Gigenzer in his book, *The Sense of Being Stared At.* "No educated person wants to be thought superstitious, precisely because being superstitious undermines his or her claim to be educated. To go against this taboo involves a serious loss of intellectual standing, a relegation to the ranks of the uneducated, the childish and superstitious. In England, skepticism about anything historically associated with witchcraft, including psychic powers, has dominated the scientific and academic worlds for generations. Whatever intellectuals may think in private, skepticism is usually an integral part of their public image."

I didn't understand it at the time, but when I wrote that poem for Brittany Murphy, it was in subconscious defiance of that skepticism which still dominates today. The same skepticism that has defined the livelihoods of generations of women and told them what they intuit shouldn't matter or carry any weight. Writing about Brittany's death and the lives and deaths of hundreds of actresses whose stories had never been told or were co-opted from them was an act of resistance, of protest against the oppression of women's voices in totality. Through my writing, I was able to give voice to those who had been literally and metaphorically silenced, myself included, giving our lives real substance and dimension beyond what has been projected. *Dark Sparkler* wasn't just a book, it was a record of women as mass casualties, a dissenting opinion on the value of women's voices both spoken and heard—a feminist reckoning of the entertainment industry and our history. Is it any wonder this kind of power aggregated from an intuitive process—especially that of women—is something we have long tried to diminish and condemn?

Our inner voice is so powerful, so meaningful, whole institutions have worked to snuff it out in order to protect self-interests and not rock the status quo's boat. When it comes to making decisions, whether creative or practical, listening to our intuition raises eyebrows; it is something we've chalked up to ethereality, ungrounded and unsupported by facts. "Can We Rely on Our Intuition?" read the doubtful headline of a 2019 article in *Scientific American* which suggests that as the world becomes more complex, making decisions becomes harder. "Is it best to depend on careful analysis or to trust your gut?"

The devaluing of our intuitive processes dates back as far as recorded civilization goes. The Greek goddess Hecate could see the past, present, and future all at once—a psychic intuitive associated with spells and magic. But Hecate's meaning has been warped through the years, most notably in Shakespeare's *Macbeth* where she is reenvisioned as an ominous figure using her powers to delight in Macbeth's suffering. The wise woman reimagined a crone, a word which is derived from the French *carrion* meaning disagreeable woman. What women intuited in their gut was, indeed, disagreeable for most of history, from the Middle Ages through the Renaissance, and was seen as a direct threat to the ruling monarchical world. "We have repeatedly called attention to the basic psychic fact that the human consciousness is experienced as 'masculine,' and that the masculine has identified itself with consciousness and its growth wherever a patriarchal world has developed," wrote psychologist, philosopher, and student of Carl Jung, Erich Neumann, in his compendium on feminine archetypes, *The Great Mother*. If conscious, rational thought is associated with the masculine, then unconscious, emotional thought which houses our intuitive intelligence is seen as feminine, and therefore, less than—inferior.

The most famous disagreeability on women's part has come in the form of hearing an inner voice and then following it. Most famously, Joan of Arc heard voices attributed to God, but which were more likely a disguise for her own inner divinity. She followed that voice which led to the French army's victory in the Hundred Years War, and the end of that war was a triumph, but a woman listening to and acting upon her gut was not. She was branded a heretic and burned alive at the age of nineteen.

Two hundred years later, women were still being burned at the stake, or close to it, for tapping into what their intuition might be telling them. Margery Kempe was a religious mystic in the 1300s known as the Weeping Mystic who took pilgrimages all over the world in the name of what voices were telling her, as did Hildegard of Bingen (c. 1098–1179), a polymath who used hearing voices as a way to forge religious abolition for the women of her time.

(Bingen invented a second alphabet called *litterae ignotae* in which she could speak in code to increase solidarity among her nuns.) Records of ordinary women listening to their intuition, or the voices they might have heard in their heads, does not exist outside of the stories of recognized and approved mystics and saints, ones that could be canonized by the Catholic Church, such as Teresa of Ávila (c. 1515–1582). It was fine for women to hear a calling, sometimes, as long as it was in the eyes—and in the voice—of the Lord.

Women hearing voices was once again weaponized with the advent of psychiatry in the nineteenth century as they turned from consulting their priests to a new form of doctors: psychiatrists. The French philosopher Jules Ferry (c. 1832–1885) was quoted as saying, "Women must belong to science or else they belong to the church," and as evidenced by history, women had to belong to *something*, lest they belong to the devil. Ferry's proclamation of women's intuition was part of a century's worth of torturous experimentation on their minds and bodies in the name of science—science that is now considered to be extreme exploitation bordering on sexual abuse. Women hearing voices was no longer the Lord's work but mental illness, with diagnoses such as *hysteria* making their debut. The neurologist Jean-Martin Charcot (c. 1825–1893) would famously conduct public viewings of experimentations on female patients under the guise of research in front of audiences of male peers, such as bloodletting and so called Scottish showers, whereby women were made to undergo hot and cold douching in order to shock them out of psychophysiological states. It wasn't until the feminist movement of the 1970s and the

creation of the Hearing Voices Movement (HVM) that
what women heard and potentially intuited was given any
kind of respect or nuanced definition.

It is almost impossible to repudiate the history books
when it comes to women and the voices they heard and
why, because it's hard to trust those who have historically
been in control of the narrative. Who can ever truly say
what was or wasn't the reason behind what women were
hearing and following, what was or wasn't mental illness,
auditory hallucinations, the side effects of psychiatric experimentation, or what was or wasn't, simply, intuition? Much
of the records on women's lived experiences are written,
studied, and translated by men with allegiances to a religion
or their budding scientific careers. What little first-person
accounts we do have by women on the voices they heard
often read like the declarations of a hostage. Throughout
history, women—who had no formal education until the
1800s—had to entrust the interpretation of what they were
hearing by societies that did not have their best interests
in mind, that often saw them as threats. It was the male
priests they had to confide in, the doctors who were doing
the diagnosing, and the historians who got to define them.
The absence of intuition as a recognized mainstream
form of understanding is, in large part, because "careful
analysis" (as that *Scientific American* article put it) is seen as
the de facto decision-making process, leaving intuition's
credibility to be undermined and further smeared. Even
now, most people associate intuitive intelligence and listening to an inner voice with new age woo-woo spiritu-

alism, founded in pseudoscience alone. Today, if a woman speaks about something she feels as fact, she is branded too emotional, hysterical, crazy, uninformed. According to Gigerenzer, it is flat out wrong and an excuse to ignore the bigger picture. "It's important to distinguish between the world where you can calculate the risks, and other situations where you can't do that. Calculating the risk would be the case if you were playing roulette, or the lottery, where all probabilities are known, all possible outcomes are known, all consequences are known. But in many situations, there is uncertainty where you cannot know the probabilities—not even estimate them. And moreover, you can't know all the future states of the world."

He goes on to shed light on the value of leaning on our intuition as much as we lean on analysis in situations of uncertainty, when a definitive conclusion is not possible and where options are available. How can you know for sure the exact right person to marry? Or the absolute correct sole person to hire? You can estimate as closely as you can, with analysis, but that still may not give you everything you need. "Precise calculations are an illusion in this situation," continues Gigerenzer. "What's useful is heuristics that are robust, rules of thumb that have a good chance to hit, as opposed to a calculation that overfits the past."

Intuition is a gift, something we should work toward understanding and using as much as we do our rational thought. What would women's mental health and women's connections to their own inner voices have looked like had they been free of such long-term oppression? Would Brittany Murphy's destiny have been different? During my research of her life, I discovered that, just like me, she loved to write poetry. This detail remains a small ghost that wanders through me from time to time. I can't help but wonder if Brittany had privately felt the way I had, all those years we crossed paths, if we had been sisters in our suppression, both quietly longing to break free from the labels carried since childhood.

To this day, when I see her name or face pop up in cultural references or articles, I don't think of her as the girl who stole all the scenes in the classic film *Clueless*—though she was. I think of her as the girl who didn't make it out the way I did. I see her as an archive of my former life: a reminder of who I once was and who she will never get to be. I may even see her now as the face of that apparition who sits down inside me when I'm getting ready to write, an amulet of my intuition, forever freed of our industry— the one who disappears, over and over again, so that something new may be reborn of us both.

Five years after Brittany Murphy's voice whispered those two words to me in passing at an audition, she was gone forever. After days of letting my anxiety play out in the forms it needed to, that one line of poetry dancing around in my head, I sat down at my kitchen table and prepared to listen to a voice so powerful, not even a medieval neurologist could douche it out of me. Writing requires an almost complete suspension of intellectual thought and a total immersion into the application of all our intuitive senses, all at work at once. To be a good writer with not just something important to say but in which it is well said, this must become a practice you master: to hone the way you enter into and stay within a creative moment. "Intuition is not to be consulted once and then forgotten," writes Clarissa Pinkola Estés in *Women Who Run With the Wolves*. "It is not disposable. It is to be consulted at all steps along the way, whether the woman's work be clashing with a demon in the interior, or completing a task in the outer world."

I put my fingers on the keyboard, and I look up and out at my view of Los Angeles, the Hollywood sign far in the distance, like pearly white teeth resting in the mouth of Los Feliz. I let my mind find the words and my body guide their transcription. When I'm writing, I never go back and reread immediately; I let it all come out first while a single song plays on repeat for hours at a time in the background. There are still songs to this day I only ever associate with a piece of writing I wrote while listening to it. For Brittany's poem, it was Yo La Tengo's "Hyas and Stenorhynchus." For this essay, it is Bibio's "It Was Willow." I am totally and completely isolated from the world, tapping into what my body and my mind are creating together. Once I'm finished, I'll go through and read it, tighten phrases and imagery, sharpen simile and metaphor, fine-tuning it all until its serration can be felt in my blood as if inflicted. I breathe. My body releases. My stomach unfurls, my toes search the ground. I print what I've written, one step closer to real. My fingers run across its surface.

It is a gift—the result of my voice, heard, and the evidence of how it manifests—that I'm now ready to let go of and give away to you.

# Practicing the Quiet

*By Amy Poehler*
*Actress and Director*

We all remember the famous scene in *Goodfellas*: Karen
(Lorraine Bracco) visits mobster Jimmy (Robert De Niro)
and asks him for help. Her husband, Henry (Ray Liotta),
has come upon hard times, and the guys in the mob don't
trust him anymore. Jimmy offers Karen money and some
fancy Dior dresses and motions for her to take a walk down
the alley and head around the corner. He kisses her and
tells her, "Don't worry." She starts to walk, passing busted
pinball machines and empty industrial storefronts.

She seems confused at first and turns to notice Jimmy
watching her intently. She becomes concerned. So do we.
Jimmy urges her to continue around the corner, and against
her better judgment, she does. Slightly aggravated and buzz-
ing with fear, Karen comes upon two men in a dark and
dusty room. They are moving around large boxes. They
are large themselves. One of them shushes the other as she
approaches. She takes this in.

She looks back at Jimmy, who urges her again to make the turn into the room. Her fear finally runs the show. She lifts up her chin and hustles back to her car. "No, Jimmy, I'm in a hurry," she says. "My mom's watching the kids. I gotta get home." She peels out and drives back to her house, sobbing. Her husband greets her, gun in hand. He asks her what happened. She doesn't know how to answer. "I just got scared," she says. "Nothing happened. I just got scared."

This is what intuition looks and feels like. Small steps down a sketchy alley until your body tells you *Run*.

I was in college in Boston in 1991, walking down a tree-lined street just as the sun had dipped down for the night. I was feeling good. Free. My hands swinging by my side and my face up and open, watching the moonlight stream between the map of trees above me. I had just helped some college kids coax a cat out of a tree, and I was thinking about that cat and those kids when I heard fast footsteps behind me. I didn't turn around or get scared or even stop my stride. I assumed it was someone out for a jog so I moved to my right to let them pass. Instead, a person came up behind me and slipped their arms under my swinging ones. My arms went up over my head, locked in by a much stronger set of arms. I remember my brain thinking of a half nelson, a wrestling term that describes a specific hold between an opponent's arms. I might have laughed. I was relaxed. I must know this person and these arms; they must be just playing around. When I turned around, I saw the face of a man I did not know.

This is the part in the movie where we pause. Or better yet, we rewind. We watch me walk backward, getting smaller in the frame until all that is left is an empty street. We press Play and watch me walk again, this time looking only at my face. We zoom in. We notice I am not noticing. We become aware of how unaware this girl with the swinging arms really is.

I grew up in the 80s, an era when adults were messy in real time, and social media wasn't there to memorialize your mistakes. We kids let ourselves into our houses when we got home from school and pretended to be adults until the real ones came back. Adults didn't check our search history or take us to therapy. Nobody was watching, so we watched what we wanted. We watched *Death Wish* and *The Exorcist* and *Behind the Green Door.* We saw our friends' parents drunk. Our teachers passed out in class. Our restaurant managers started fistfights with fry cooks. There was a reason the deeply talented, depressive Charles M. Schulz excluded adults from his Peanuts cartoons. We all knew that most of these people were full of shit. We nodded in unison during the Charlie Brown Christmas specials when the adult voices were portrayed as plaintive trombones. *Wha wha wha wha wha.* They weren't saying anything important. Our parents never came to our schools. Even the best ones. The only time they arrived was to deliver bad news or baked goods. Parents went to work, and kids went to school, and we didn't really share how either was going.

And yet, danger loomed all around us as a mix of kidnappings and devil worship. After-school specials warned

us not to hitchhike and kept us up at night with visions of
getting into cars with no handles on the inside. We drank
from milk cartons with missing kids our age plastered across
them. We went from No Nukes to No Means No to Just
Say No. At the same time, we were taught to be strong and
independent women. Express yourself! Ask for the beef!
Wear sneakers during your commute, and don't let anyone
call you cute. Play through the pain. It was this complicated soup of self-sabotage that was served up as a way to
*listen to one's inner voice.* We were told to get quiet and listen to our heart, but it was hard to do that while we were
encouraged to roar.

As a grown-ass woman, I now know how impossible a
task it is to hold these two truths at the same time. How
hard it is to take up your rightful space while still being
hyperaware of how loud you are being. As I've gotten wiser
over the years, I've learned that the quiet space is what we've
all been overlooking. The very rare moment when our
butterfly brain lands on a leaf and we are connected to the
present moment for even just a few wing flaps. The quiet
space is also the trick, the prize. It helps me read people in
a loud room. It helps me understand my son even when he
is not speaking. It helps me chip away at the lifelong practice of figuring out what I want first. It feels earned, this
quiet. The quiet burns the rest away, and all that is left is
the good part. The honest and real part. That's why it is so
hard to access, because one must sit in a fire to get there.

As usual, the Native Americans understood this first, and
I often find myself thinking of this Lakota prayer:

*Teach me how to trust*
*My heart,*
*My mind,*
*My intuition,*
*My inner spirit,*
*The senses of my body,*
*The blessings of my spirit.*
*Teach me to trust these things*
*So that I may enter my Sacred Space*
*And love beyond my fear,*
*And thus Walk in Balance*
*With the passing of each Glorious Sun.*

I love this because it reminds me that I have a body, which my brain would like me to forget. And also, let's get real, I love a list.

I also think of this.

In Sanskrit, there is the concept of *maya*, which comes from ancient Hindu philosophy. It's a term that translates to *magic, illusion,* and *things not being what they seem.* Freeing ourselves from this veil can be our spiritual path and can be done with stillness, concentration, and prayer.

I love this because it reminds me that going inward is the best path. And also, let's get real, I love a map.

So you get the point. We have to be quiet. And listen. Go slow. Keep checking in with that quiet space inside us and what comes from it.

So let's return. Press Play and we're back to the scene with the tree-lined street, back to my arms locked up high above my head by a man I do not know. And my body does what my brain refuses to do. It reacts. It bucks and tries to get away, and I stumble and fall. My body is the one that says *Run, run, run*. Not my brain, which hangs out in the lab like some computer nerd trying to figure out what equation they got wrong while the zombies are breaking down the door. It is my body that is the hero. The star. It releases adrenaline as I fall on my face and then scramble to my feet. It is my body that makes me turn around and see the man. A white man with brown hair who has eyes that seem much too big and much too open. It is my body that feels he must be on something. I increase my heart rate and pump my legs. I get up my stairs, up to my apartment, up to my bedroom where I sit for hours talking to roommates in an attempt to flatten it all out. I file all the hard lessons into small folders in my mind. Never walk that open and carefree again, I tell myself. Never trust the sound of running behind you. Never save cats.

As a culture, we are drawn to people who have listened to their gut and come out the winner because of it. The woman who has a bad feeling and doesn't get on the plane. The mother who knows something is wrong with her child. The CEO who gambles with their company while everyone tells them they are crazy. What part of these decisions are luck or just timing? Or is it just God's Great Big Plan? What part is instinct, and what part is intuition? Do we even know the difference between the two? Where intuition is the ability to know and understand something without conscious thought, instinct is far more primal, a fixed pattern of behavior that happens in any animal when prompted to do so. Intuition depends on instinct plus time, and feelings plus experience, like what happened to me that day I got away from a bad stranger.

It was a combination of many things that got me home safely that night. But what would've happened if my body had chosen not to listen to itself that night? What do you do if you dip inside your own head and hear nothing? What if you dig deep and all you find in the quiet space is an empty room? What if you ask yourself what to do and all that comes back is the sound of a dog barking nearby? Dead air and static. The wrong kind of quiet space. The dull nothing where little is felt and less is known. What then? How can you learn to listen?

It's been thirty years since that night on the street with the stranger, and I am driving in Los Angeles, a city I am frankly still surprised I live in. I am more practiced at the quiet. Better at the listening. And many decades later, aware of how surprising people can be. Wary of new people but even more suspicious of nice ones. My Irish grandmother used to say, "Strangers should be a little strange." I understand this better now. I used to take great pride in my ability to intuit a person or a behavior, but now I know that I am a bent weather vane. Sometimes my North points a little West, and the shadows it casts make it difficult for me to see when I am moving in the wrong direction and making the wrong assumptions.

I drive past a young woman on the median holding a sign. I can't see what it says, but I clock a few things fast. She is young and slight and trying to get past a man. He has a wide-legged stance and seems to be blocking her way. It's hot outside, that white, bright California light that makes everything feel like an operating room. This man is young, like her. He has his eyes closed, and his hands are open and faced up to the sky. It looks like he is waiting to catch something. A break, perhaps? Next to him is a sign and what looks like flowers. Perhaps that is what he is selling, but I can't tell if they are together or if he is bothering her. I drive past them in five seconds, and my mind is whirling with questions. Are they in love? Does she need help? What is my voice telling me?

I decide to circle around, to give this voice and my brain and my eyes time to interpret—to understand. This time I see more clues. Context clues. She is pregnant. They are talking, interacting. She seems irritated or maybe nervous. They don't see me.

I pull over and roll down my window. Immediately the cars behind me start to honk, and the self-righteous indignation I feel gives me the signal that I think I am *doing a good thing*. I clock this. I motion the woman to come toward my car. I ask her if she is okay. I ask her if the man is bothering her. Her answers are vague and detached, like she isn't in her own body. She has soft brown eyes and holds her belly while she talks about being evicted from her apartment. I ask her if she is living on the streets or in a shelter, and then the conversation turns to her family, who doesn't help her and never has. The beeping behind me is loud and incessant. I look again at him and at her. I try to see if they are a unit. I try to see if this is a bad thing or a good thing, knowing it is probably a complicated mix of both. I give her money. I drive away. I pull over a few blocks later and try to dig deep and understand what I am feeling. Let the quiet space take over so I can see what to take away from this interaction. I'm agitated. Numb. Savior-like. Ashamed of my assumptions. All of the things.

There is no easy answer here, and my intuition mixed with my quiet gives me no clear sense of what I saw. The feeling is an itch I can't reach. Sometimes we don't get the whole story, and we are left with the uncomfortable middle mess. The nauseous feeling of something missed. We are like Karen in *Goodfellas*. We know something felt wrong, but the discomfort comes from not being able to figure it out.

Each day in the movie of my own life, I get better at knowing what the main character is going to do, even if the doing has an outcome I did not expect. Let's just say I prepare to be surprised. I have a saying I use often: *Good for you, not for me.* It's a way of saying I'm happy for other people's choices, but I am very clear about which ones do not suit me at all. The main character in my life has an idea of who she is and what she likes. She will cook for the people she loves. She will not go to haunted houses. She will stand up for her friends. She will keep her head down when rowdy teens get on the subway. She will pick her battles and always watch carefully.

She is a mess of contradictions. She would never walk down a street at night swinging her arms. She will never let them take the swing out of her arms. She would never follow a guy down an alley for a free coat. She will follow a guy for less. She will do it wrong and do it right in a thousand different ways. Over and over. All the while, she will listen for the little sounds deep down inside her. The space that holds a small humming music box with a twirling ballerina inside, just waiting to be opened. Its quiet tinkling the softest messages that our girl can hear if she'll only pause to listen.

# Mirrors

By Ayanna Pressley
*Congresswoman and Movement Builder*

Do you ever think about what a mirror really is? How it works? The reality is no two are exactly the same. As you move through the world, each image reflected to you will appear slightly differently. When rays of light hit rough surfaces, they bounce the light back in all directions. This is called diffuse reflection. Metal and glass, meanwhile, are very smooth and reflect light back in a different way. They offer a closer measure of what's represented in front of the surface, but it's still not a perfect replica.

Growing up in Chicago, my mother was my mirror, reflecting to me and the world all the light embodied within her. I was constantly by the side of a woman who was steady, fierce, loving, and human. She was my shero. She gave me my roots and my wings. She taught me that our job and our work are two separate things. Our job—and she had many—is what pays the bills. Our Work—with a capital *w*—is the collective work of liberation and upliftment of community.

She loved me fiercely. When I was a child, she did not read me bedtime stories. She read me the words of Barbara Jordan and Shirley Chisholm. She ached for me to see in myself deep potential, value, self-worth, and dignity. She sought to instill in me from an early age a counternarrative. She knew that the world writ large does not value the humanity and fullness of Black women. That we are often portrayed as a narrow reflection of who we are, filtered through a prism of outside expectations, biases, and shortcomings. But in our home and in her loving arms, she anchored me to a vision of my power.

My mother took exception when people used nicknames for me. My name, Ayanna, translates to *beautiful flower*, and my mother would tell me that she had given me the name for a reason: so that I would never be without the affirmation of my beauty and worth. Later in life, she routinely gifted me flowers to wear on my lapel, a physical reflection of the name she had given me.

The experience of learning to see myself through my mother's eyes, with the intentionality and fullness she sought to impart, was not always an easy one. I often found myself—and still do—in spaces and moments that reflected a broken image, where my body, the way that I simply showed up in the world, was seen as disruptive, deserving of criticism, somehow inadequate. In those moments, I had to fight to remember my mother's mirror: that who I authentically was would always be enough.

My mother did not hesitate to prepare me with the armor I needed to navigate the world. But she also passed on—in word and deed—an innate understanding that embracing my joy was, in and of itself, an act of liberation. In a world that would place on my shoulders many expectations, what would matter most was that I found my way and defined my own path, one foot in front of the next. What mattered was that when I looked in the mirror, I would not see an image refracted by the lens of society, I would see a full, deserving, purposeful, and deeply loved woman. I would see Sandy Pressley's daughter.

There is a small mirror in my office that I always look into before I head out to make a speech on the House floor or testify in committee. As a congresswoman, there's a practical reality to stepping out of my office door each day: my appearance matters. I check for lipstick on my teeth or smudged makeup from the sticky DC heat. But that's not why I started this ritual. My mirror, my intuition, guides me through the world all women must navigate when we open our door each day to the outside world which filters our image and actions through the fractious perspective of others' lived experiences. On any given matter, on any given day, my words—always with consistent purpose and intent—will land differently on any two sets of ears. The mirrors that refract through the lens of a shutter, the C-SPAN camera, and the livestream does not accurately reflect me. They catch the angles of rough surfaces, creating a diffuse reflection. They will not see me through the mirror I see myself in but that of their own making.

I have always loved language. I learned early on from a church pew the gift and true discipline of delivering a word. Of meeting the moment and offering folks language to describe their discomfort, soften the edges of a harsh reality, or lift their hearts as they move through the day. Some words, when strung together just right, in the moment they are most needed, can reflect something real and true. Words can hold together a shared sentiment that unifies people who see the world and move through it in deeply different ways. Sometimes we catch a glimpse of those moments where we collectively see a crisp image of what's in front of us and what's possible.

And yet, the goal is often not to peer into the same mirror at the same moment and see the same image reflected. The world is too multidimensional, people are too multidimensional, to fit such a limited view. That would overlook the complexity of who we each are and how the world has shaped us. The narrative we have crafted, from moments of adversity and moments of true joy and love. What we are after is shared purpose, not perfection. My mother set me on a path to define the way the world saw me, but her primary goal was that I define the way I see myself—that my first instinct when I look in that mirror before leaving my office is not one of judgment but one of affirmation, purpose, and perseverance.

She instilled in me a deep sense of empathy but cautioned that that empathy must come with some armor. It is too easy to elevate each person I cross paths with, to put them in the front row of my heart regardless of their intent. To give the comments of a childhood friend the same weight as someone who wishes my family harm or hurls sharp words at me. After all, most humans are seeking to be heard and seen fully. Whether possible or not, a part of us wants others to see us the way we see ourselves—to be seen, heard, and valued for precisely who we are. But that experience can be vanishingly elusive—the good inevitably accompanied by the hateful—and we must learn to don our armor and choose which reflections we allow into our hearts.

As a woman, I have leaned into my intuition by defining my own mirrors. They don't always show me an image I'm comfortable with, but they reflect my truth. That counsel provides the strength to step into an often-unwelcoming world and manifest my full self.

As I navigate the machinations of my daily life and fight for the most vulnerable, those left out and left behind, I find myself shoulder to shoulder with far too many who cast aside those mirrors, push through eye contact, and presume their mirror is the only one through which we must all see. But that is no way to move in this world with purpose. To see others fully, we have to first fully see ourselves. Our whole selves. Each day, we must choose to go in one direction—to see one single version of ourselves as truth. We see the direction of weariness and indifference, or we see the direction of hope and justice. To know the direction you must choose, follow what your intuition is telling you is staring back at you. Lock eyes with her through the glass, and commit to exactly what you see reflected back.

# Gut Feelings

*By Samantha Irby*
*Essayist*

In 1989 my pals and I got dropped off at the Evanston I Movie Theater (there was no Evanston II, weird), with enough money to get matinee tickets to see *The Little Mermaid*. I was nine years old and had decided it was my favorite movie of all time. We got a large popcorn, with instructions to call my mom from the pay phone (Do you even know what that is?) in the lobby as soon as the credits rolled.

We rushed into the hallway, breathless with joy and excitement from the movie, and as I fished in my pocket for a quarter, one of my giggling, chattering preteen friends conspiratorially whispered, "Should we sneak into another movie?" My hands went clammy, and I started to sweat as I shook my head no (I shook it so aggressively that it wasn't just *no*, it was *ABSOLUTELY NOT*), but it was too late: my friends were already tiptoeing down the hall toward another darkened theater to see my favorite cult classic horror flick, *I Have No Idea Because I Sat on a Bench near the Women's Bathroom for Two Hours Nervously Grinding My Teeth into Stumps*. Have you seen that one before? Look for it next time you're at Blockbuster.

Something inside me knew they were going to get caught. I just knew they were gonna be dragged out by their braids and ponytails, kicking and screaming through a trail of spilled soda and popcorn, shrieking that they needed just five more minutes to see who the killer was, as the beleaguered theater manager signaled to the Sno-Caps dealer on duty to call the police. As I sat there silently for an hour watching the door—my stomach roiling and churning with fear, sweat-slick palms restless inside my corduroy pockets—I watched as an usher finally hustled those red-faced, embarrassed criminals out into the light of the lobby and told them to either buy a ticket or leave. I felt triumphant because I was a little asshole weasel who loved being good and right, but also because I was too terrified of punishment or public humiliation to break even one arbitrary rule. As I watched them each call their mothers to come pick them up (and take them to prison), I felt less bad about being neither fun nor cool and more resolute about my position as a strict law abider than ever. But what saved me from embarking on a life of racketeering that day? Was it intuition, or was it anxiety?

*LOL it was anxiety.* I have been anxious since the moment I understood that being alive—that the act of living—is dangerous, that everything on this planet is conspiring at all hours of the day to hurt or maim or kill you. I taught myself that the only way to move through the world unscathed is to recognize every interaction as a potential threat and every inanimate object as your worst enemy. So, I guess, since kindergarten? First grade???

I'm not sure when my anxiety prompted me to start unnecessarily taking the long way in life, like literally going way out of my way to avoid terrible potholes on a street that I know all too well might fuck up my car tires. (*WHO DOES THIS?!* I do.) Or getting to the airport three hours early to pee, then sit, then pee some more, then rest, then flip through all the magazines at Hudson News, then pee again, then watch the two other flights leaving from my gate board and leave, then pee one more time, just in case.

My anxiety has always kept me prepared for any possible outcome. Take into consideration, for instance, the contents of my bag: a wallet, a book in case I get bored, a charger in case my phone dies, a backup charger in case my original charger wasn't charged as much as it should've been, a variety of medicines (something for allergies, something for pain, something for diarrhea, something for painful diarrhea), an extra pair of glasses (just in case the ones currently on my face...................evaporate while I'm wearing them???), hand sanitizer, a ChapStick, a second ChapStick, a third ChapStick (I promise I need this many), and should I maybe bring an extra book in case I get stuck somewhere for long enough that I finish the first one? I'm not a doomsday prepper, I just get, oh, I don't know, extremely uneasy and like to take precautions.

It is this uneasiness that helped me nurture such a wild and fucked-up imagination—an imagination that can be great for writing, when it gets its shit together, but also an imagination that can imagine the fuck out of any possible scenario in any given situation, many of which are doomful. I don't know why I didn't get in the car after that party. Did I instinctively know there were a lot of drunk drivers out there just waiting to paint the highway with my entrails? Or do I just not like to be behind the wheel after 4:00 p.m. during the winter months when it gets pitch-black by dinnertime? We'll never know! Did a little voice inside save me from wasting an entire paycheck on scratch-off lottery tickets, or was that caution a product of an over-protective mother who spent hours on end warning me of the myriad horrors that could befall me anytime? Hmm, I'm not sure I can say!

You know how there are some people who, you know, spend a lot of drunk time reminiscing fondly on their wild and carefree youths? I do not have any of those recollections. My brain is crowded with scary-seeming playground activities I walked away from and low-stakes risks I refused to take. I think I was always afraid of really letting go and looking stupid or getting into the kind of trouble my mom didn't have enough money to get me out of. I think when you come from a family that centers problems as its narrative rather than solutions as its mission (these are designations I just made up because *We were broke and uninsured* doesn't have a zippy ring to it), extreme caution is just sorta baked into the cake of who you are.

I grew up believing risk was only for the rich. I understood very early that there was no bank account or credit card available to me to get me out of a jam, or fix something I'd broken, or supply any kind of rescue I might need, which resulted in the kind of person who fixates on the consequence of the consequence of the consequence of every single decision I am faced with, either high stakes or low. It's so I can game out whether or not I'll be able to save my own ass if things go haywire. I've made a ton of shitty choices, of course, but even those were never the shittiest choices I could have made. There are so many doors I never peeked behind and unlocked phones I never scrolled through!

At first, channeling all of my existential anxieties into writing jokes on the internet was a good and cheap substitute for the therapy I couldn't afford and absolutely could have used while trying to navigate the choppy waters of trying to find strangers on the internet to have sex with. In the olden days, venturing out on a date looked like me meeting up in a dark bar near my apartment with some dude I messaged for a week on eHarmony, only to register his disappointment when he saw me, just as he registered mine. We would suffer together through polite small talk and bad cocktails until parting ways, mutually pretending we might see each other again. We wouldn't, and I would then head home, feeling like the loneliest girl in the world, to smoke some weed and listen to an Amy Winehouse song on repeat until I fell asleep. (For the record, "Wake Up Alone" is the perfect accompaniment for a post-date sulk alone in your room, should you ever need one.)

I was very hard on myself and ruthless when it came to picking at my scabs and berating myself for my flaws. I'd sit there in the dark like, "You're stupid, you're ugly, why did you wear that shirt? Did he think your jokes were dumb?

Is he texting his friends right now about all the loser shit you said?" and on and on, while some forlorn chanteuse (sometimes it was Tori Amos or Beth Gibbons or Aimee Mann) warbled in the background as I cried.

But when I started blogging (Do you even know what that is anymore?), I realized that I could take all that humiliated angst, take all of my prickly uncertainty and fear of the outside world, and pour it into my battered old laptop, alchemizing those icky, skin-crawly feelings into words that made me laugh and that I hoped would make my stupid friends laugh, too. There's something medicative about taking something that makes me feel like garbage and churning it through my interior joke machine until it becomes something I can laugh at. In a way, this is how I learned to use all my childhood anxiety as something useful: a terrible feeling that starts out in my gut repurposed on the page to make people laugh their own guts out.

Intuition isn't a word that would've naturally occurred to me to use (it feels woo-woo and fruity, a word that someone who is more spiritual and tuned into complex emotions than I am gets to use) to describe this process of getting these stories out of my body and into the eyes and ears of other people where they can't hurt me, but that's what it is, right? No one ever told me to start working my stuff out on the page. I didn't know anyone personally who had figured out that repurposing their trauma in this specific way was beneficial to them and advised me to try it; I didn't have an example of a writer for whom the public vomiting of their innermost thoughts had proven to be a healthy coping mechanism, but something made me borrow a laptop and see what kind of magic I could make. And, after a while, doing so felt really good. My knee-jerk response is to snark that I started squeezing jokes out of my pain because I wanted attention, or I wanted to show off, but maybe my gut knew that it was deeper than that. I have an instinct for what will make people laugh or, at the very least, what will make people laugh at me. Intuition is part of my interior joke machine; it's second nature that, as I feel my skin crawling due to some hell of my own creation, my brain says, *This absolutely sucks, but it's gonna make an incredible story.*

As I transitioned from blogs to books (or, as I like to think of them, *printed-out blogs*), my process changed. Where blogging was like a short, stream of consciousness diary entry, I feel like the things I put in a book should be a little bit more curated. And special. I mean, as special as *Let me describe my diarrhea to you* can possibly be. Also, I feel anxious about charging money for the pleasure of reading about my bottomless pit of neuroses, so I want to make sure my trash feels worth fifteen whole dollars.

It typically goes one of two ways. An idea strikes me and I think, *Okay, I can wring three thousand hilarious words out of that.* Or, I find myself in................a situation. Like, my card gets declined in front of a celebrity I'm casually trying to impress, or I get turned away from a restaurant for not being dressed nicely enough. I'm not a writer who walks around with a well-worn Moleskine in her bag (God, how I wish I was that type of writer!), so if I'm not near a computer, or if I'm sitting in front of a computer with twenty-seven tabs open to gossip websites and don't feel like doing any meaningful work, I'll find my shitty old phone and text myself a series of notes I will immediately flush out of my brain and forget about entirely.

When the time comes to actually do the writing part and my stomach is in a knot because I blew through the deadline three weeks ago (*ahem*, sorry, Amber!), I'll sit at my computer and put a song on repeat in my headphones (something gentle that borders on depressing and doesn't have too many distracting words or a beat that will make me want to shoulder dance in my orthopedic desk chair; I will use basically any excuse not to work) with a Diet Coke and a bag of dry cereal, then make notes on whatever scrap of paper is handy. I like to work out the ending first, or at least have one in mind, so I have a destination to write to. It stresses me out not to know where I'm going! I use the GPS to get to the grocery store!!!!!!!

I refuse to do any research beyond a little light googling, so I only write about shit I know about. Being fact-checked gives me heartburn: once I mentioned Lifetime Movies in an essay, theoretically, as a concept, and I got a note from the fact-checker that was like *If this story took place in 19—, Lifetime Movies didn't exist then*, and I broke out in a full-body sweat, like I'd just been caught cheating on the bar exam.

Mistakes make me feel like a bad person, which is how you know that *writing as cheap therapy* I mentioned earlier is absolutely not working. Okay, so let's say I'm writing about a *situation* that would make an interesting story to tell to a stranger. First, I gotta relive the experience in my mind, which is harrowing. I can't tell you what I had

for dinner last night (pesto, maybe?), but I can recall for
you, in excruciating minute-by-minute detail, every embarrassing thing that has ever happened to me since my
brain was fully formed and capable of tucking it away in
my secret shame corner.

Next, I jot down the big beats on my scratch paper:

-I was 19, wait a second, no, I was 27
-We were in a basement, I think? Maybe a rec room,
  did Anna's dad call it a rec room or a den?
-Can't believe how wasted we were, *SHEESH*
-A bunch of girls giggling like idiots, prank calling
  our friends, ordering pizzas
-Was I sad that day? I'm pretty sure I was sad before
  I got there
-Don't forget the part about my boss yelling at me
  about something dumb
-I laughed so hard I peed on the floor, everyone else
  stopped laughing
-Had to take a cab home wearing no pants
-Was that driver gonna kill me? Why am I such a
  fucking fool?
-Absolutely banged the cab driver that night, I won-
  der what he's up to now?

That may or may not be a true story about the time I
might or might not have invited a cab driver into my bed
as my urine-soaked jeans sat steaming in a pile on the floor
next to my bed, but that is loosely how I would structure
an essay if it was.

Whatever jitters or trepidation I had about not having

something to write—or accidentally writing something terrible nobody wants to read—subsides after I write my little notes, and then it's time to relax. Nothing can hurt me now that I have a handful of semiconnected fragments that I'll hopefully be able to stitch together to make something not-bad. Now I get to look at shit on the internet for hours while a blank document sits in an open tab, taunting me. *I WIN.*

I don't know why I always put off the actual writing of the thing, because I truly do feel relieved once it's out of my head and onto the page. I can torment myself for years, turning a weird interaction over and over in my brain, torturing myself with thoughts on situations I can't change, but as soon as I vomit it out onto a page, I start feeling better about whatever it is. The thing about vomit, though, is that sometimes it stinks and splashes on things you don't want it to, like the other people at that party. Or the guy driving that cab. I make it a point to only write about people the way I'd want someone to write about me: in unrecognizably shadowy ways while changing my name and any major physical characteristics. I've never had anyone I've written about take issue with how I wrote about them, which is good because I cry easily, and I don't know how to fucking fight.

The screaming voice in my head (loud, yet unmistakably Midwestern, so with an air of passive aggression) as I spiral before actually doing the writing sounds like:

Does anyone care about this?
Why did I agree to do this?

Nothing is gonna be as good as that one good thing
I did.
Who is gonna want to read this?
Are people gonna be mad at me?
What if this sucks?
Am I a shitty person?
I'm a fraud!
Who is this for?
Does the universe need this from me?
If this is what my intuition is, then it can go fuck itself.
Maybe I can fake my own death and get out of this.
Why don't I know more words?
Will people laugh?
Do other writers struggle like this?
Are people gonna be mad at me?
People are absolutely gonna make fun of me.
Should I have gone to college?
How many negative reviews am I gonna get?
Is this embarrassing?
Is this not embarrassing enough?
Why did I think that I could do this again?
I don't deserve to get paid for this.
How on earth did I do this the last time?
Are people gonna be mad at me?
So many people are better at this than I am.
I should just quit, right?????

*No, Sam*, I say and slap myself directly in the face. Because I know whenever I write, I'm always trying to get to the heart of what my fucking problem is. What this asshole voice is, inside me, and what it's trying to convey. I'm always in confrontation with that scared part of myself that's riddled with anxiety, in a way the real-life me could never be. And it is always some high-wire balancing act between the part of me that wants to ignore it all and the part of me that wants to write it all.

Some days, I fall to my death. Other days, I make it to the other side. No matter what, for better or for worse (usually for worse), I can trust my gut to lead the way, to the toilet or to the pen.

# Knowing

*By Huma Abedin*
*Political Strategist and Author*

My mother never seemed uncertain about anything. Ever. Whether it was faith, confidence, something innate, choice, intuition, she never second-guessed herself and never seemed to waver on anything. She trusted that she just *knew*, and she followed through on that knowing. From my earliest memories, she worked outside the home, and she also worked inside the home. Essentially, my mother was always working. It was not something I thought about very often; it was just the way it was, and I took it for granted.

When she met my father on the University of Pennsylvania campus in 1964, her initial reaction was to run from him, but something deep inside told her he was right for her. And that feeling was correct. He would become the love of her life, and the marriage they modeled for me would be one for the ages.

There were four of us kids, and we were raised in Jeddah, Saudi Arabia. My mother had already left her home and her family once as a refugee from India to Pakistan,

and she eventually found her way to a Fulbright scholar-
ship in the United States and then to Saudi Arabia when
I was two years old and still in diapers. She made that decision to give up everything familiar in her life not once,
but twice, and she later told me she just had a feeling that
it was the right thing to do.

My mother didn't teach me directly how to do things, or
act on what I felt in my gut was right, but instead she taught
me by example. Each morning before school, I awoke to
the smell of scrambled eggs, to my clothes laid out fully
ironed, before Mom got ready for her own job at the university where she taught sociology to students whose first
language wasn't English. Instead of getting frustrated at
the language divide, at forty she learned a new language
to better communicate with her class. When there was a
bake sale at school, she made brownies or a cake or a pie
from whatever ingredients she had in our cupboards. She
then sat late into the night at the dining table grading papers before starting all over again the next morning. She
rarely ever sat still. Some days, after school, my sisters and
I would stop by at her university to watch as she met with
other professors or her students, or while giving a lecture
or grading more papers.

On weekends, we would go to the old city to buy fabric, and my mother would make clothes for herself and
my sisters based on patterns she picked up from her trips
to America. I would look on with awe at the way she held
her scissors aloft, stared at the fabric spread out on the
table, then proceeded to cut through the whole cloth with
such confidence in her ability to create. She always seemed

to know the right thing to do and would always follow through on that inner knowing.

I was expected to do well in school, encouraged, sometimes lectured—even pushed—when I brought home bad grades. Yet the unsaid expectation in our house was simple: I could become whatever I wanted when I grew up, but all that was required of me was that I be educated. I didn't know then how much education was prized by the matriarchs of my family. I did not know the story of my grandmother who, at eight years of age, had demanded over a hundred years earlier to go to a formal school in India, during a time when girls in her community simply did not do things like go to school. I did not know my mother was homeschooled during her formative years and then was self-taught using her curiosity to explore books from family libraries until she ended up getting her PhD from the University of Pennsylvania. I did not know how much her being a first in achieving that kind of academic excellence was in such stark contrast to all of her immediate peers.

It was a home where I was constantly told I was loved, where I was held, where I felt protected, where I felt anything was possible in my future. It was where I was encouraged to create—to write stories, pen sappy poetry, and perform in family plays with my siblings—and sent out to make adult conversation with guests visiting from around the world, and put on the phone with airlines to book family vacations. These were things that scared me when I was little—things I didn't think that I had the ability to do at my age—but I did them with encouragement from my parents. I always knew I could run back into their arms if I got overwhelmed, but that they would always lovingly push me back out into the world once more, believing in me almost more than I believed in myself.

That was a gift, a treasured, almost too-perfect childhood. It was also a bit of a fantasy. What I was protected from was the fact that my father was ill most of my young life. To me, he was an indestructible hero, an illusion created by my mother. She did everything so we didn't notice what my father couldn't do. Because of this, all my memories of my father are frozen in time, dipped in amber and put up on a pedestal forever, while my relationship with my mother remained dynamic, filled with the push and pull that often comes in mother–daughter relationships during the friction of those turbulent adolescent years.

When I was seventeen years old, I lost my father when routine surgery for a stomach ulcer turned out to be anything but. He died a week later from multiple organ failure, and my mother lost the love of her life. For a moment in time, our roles reversed in a way I could never have anticipated. My mother simply stopped her perpetual movement, her decision-making, her work. She broke down and cried. She lay in bed for hours. Something changed in me too that day, and a voice inside propelled me into action as *her* caretaker, as the one who could step up and step in to handle the business of our household while my mother grieved.

I was able to fill the shoes of this responsibility because that innate knowing, which tells you what to do when no one else does, had been modeled to me by her. Making calls and arrangements, receiving guests, responding to condolence notes, burying my father. I became the doer, the mover, the unafraid. Soon after the funeral, on a whim more than anything else, I told my mother I wouldn't be leaving for my first year at university after all, which was now just two months away. I told her I would remain in Saudi Arabia and try and pick up the work of my father's academic journal and foundation. She didn't tell me what to do, she just said that whatever I chose, she would support me, but that I should think about it.

I made the *istikhara*, which is the prayer of intention in my faith. The word translates to *prayer of seeking counsel*, and it is a prayer Muslims make before making big life decisions. It's not meant to be a static experience. You don't just make a wish and then wait for it to come true or not. The prayer forces you to listen and to ask questions: to meditate, to contemplate, to think about your actions, your intentions and their consequences. When allowing yourself to process it all, it gives you a sense of peace and serenity. As I sat in my father's office reflecting on the decision to stay with my family or go to university, I felt something in the pit of my stomach and then heard a clear voice in my head. The pit did not feel good about sitting where I was, and the voice in my head said, simply, *Go*. It was not necessarily a physical feeling, not a tremor or a nagging, just something in that empty space in the center of me: a feeling that I needed to *move*.

One result of making the *istikhara* prayer is that it allowed for a pathway to my intuition to open—an intuition which speaks to me through a divine power. Over the years, I have learned to trust this relationship between my inner voice and this prayer, which has served me well, time and time again. Nothing about my life today would have been what it was if I hadn't first listened to "Think about it" and then heard *Go.*

When I left Saudi Arabia for America and walked into the White House as a twenty-one-year-old intern three years later, I carried the lessons my mother had modeled for me into that experience. I had applied for an internship in the White House press office because I wanted to pursue a career in journalism, but I was assigned to the First Lady's policy office instead. I called my mother from my very first cell phone to relay the news that I didn't get my first choice job, and she told me, "Sometimes plan A doesn't work out, but plan B can turn out to be just as good, if not better."

Once again, what she innately knew was right. I was also, for the first time, in the presence of a woman whose own intelligence and inner knowing reminded me so much of my mother's—an icon of women's rights around the world—Hillary Rodham Clinton.

It had been a year since the First Lady had delivered her groundbreaking speech in Beijing declaring that, "Women's rights are human rights and human rights are women's rights, once and for all." Before she made that trip in 1995 and delivered her speech, she had been told it was a risky message, perhaps even a mistake to go. But much like my mother, she just *knew* it was the right thing to do, and she followed through on that knowing. She did this fully aware of the potential consequences and political ramifications of her speech—a speech which would ultimately become a historical and revolutionary one that awakened the world to the treatment of women and girls in China.

Almost nothing that happened in her office—which we called Hillaryland—happened by chance or on a whim. Experts were consulted, research was done, meetings were hashed out and rehashed, decisions were analyzed—no one works in a vacuum in government. You are working for the American people, and so going to work every day you know the decisions you participate in, big or small, can have significant consequences. And yet still, it was so important for us to also rely on our gut—to be able to make informed decisions with sometimes difficult answers. On many predawn mornings, some colleagues would meet by the south gate and take group runs down the National Mall and back, talking about the upcom ing day or week or nothing in particular. On trips, our team would often go on long exploratory walks through cities or countrysides. I vividly remember a serene walk in an orange grove in Morocco as the First Lady talked to a friend about trying to decide whether to run for the United States Senate.

I was taught two fundamental lessons by the women who were my predecessors in Hillaryland. The first was *Fail to plan, plan to fail.* I have lived my entire professional life trying to abide by that principle, one that highlights the paramount importance of planning ahead, but which also prepares you for what to do in the event things don't turn out the way you planned. The second was to make a decision—to not be paralyzed by fear or indecision. In what were often high-pressure environments with little time, you had to decide, even if the right decision wasn't always so obvious in a complicated political and diplomatic world. You had to be so in tune with what your gut was telling you that you could access it within a millisecond.

This second lesson was, in some ways, harder to follow, because it was harder to define in practical terms. You can be academically excellent, be rational, have all the data and information on a decision at your disposal, but sometimes it comes down to the knowing: what just *feels* right. I happen to believe that following that feeling in the pit of your gut—that intuition that we all possess—is something innate, not something taught. My mother couldn't teach me how to have it, but she could show me how to find it, which she did. No matter what our relationship is or is not to intuition, we all have the ability to access it. We just need to have the courage to follow through.

There was a period of time in those White House years when I shared the same job as my colleague Allison. We were both type A personalities, both prepared to do whatever it took to get the job done, to outwork anyone else. But at the same time, we were stepping all over each other in the process; I thought *I* should be in charge, and she thought *she* should be in charge. We talked over each other, we each offered the First Lady different directions about what to do next, where we were going, what we each thought she needed. Finally, sanity (and our boss's voice) settled things between us, and we learned that our strength was not in what we had to offer separately, but in what we could achieve together. On our own, our knowledge and intuitive intelligence was strong, but as a united front we had so much more to offer. This understanding between Allison and me has forged a friendship that's lasted twenty-five years, and this mentality—a hard work ethic, guided by facts, information, and intuition—became the foundation all of us at Hillaryland were known for.

At the end of two terms of the Clinton administration, there was an informal farewell ceremony put together where awards were given out to staff members by senior staff. One of the awards was for those individuals who had served the entire consecutive eight years. The office that received the most of that award was the First Lady's office, which wouldn't surprise anyone who worked there. Ours was the kind of work ethic that came from the top down, and we worked, planned, executed, and problem-solved with such efficiency, it may have seemed easy from the outside looking in but it was anything but that. We got things done as a collective unit, and there was an intuitive rhythm to how the women in Hillaryland worked together; each of our decisions informed and impacted the other.

I have often wondered what went through the mind of my grandmother as an eight-year-old in 1910 when she demanded to be educated. Did she have a feeling? A pit in her stomach? Did she know that her journey on that rickety oxcart would change her life? And her daughter's life? And mine? Every time I imagine the roads I have traveled, the countries I have visited, the living legends I have met, the palaces I have slept in, I imagine that she did know. That she felt something big, that she dreamed of possibilities beyond her grasp. And because she allowed herself to listen to her own inner voice and follow through on what it told her, she altered our collective history.

Now at forty-six, my intuition has become a larger piece of my whole. I don't second-guess myself as much as I did a decade ago. I don't make a decision about work or something personal, then wonder if it was right or wrong or worry about the consequences. It doesn't fester in me in the way it used to. I trust that I know and what I know. It was something first modeled for me by my mother, who learned it from her own mother, just as it was handed down through the generations of the women who came before them. I took what they gave me and broadened and nurtured it in my professional life alongside women who were doing the same.

In my twenties and thirties, my insecurities, my sense of needing external approval, meant that that inner voice was often just a whisper. But one of the biggest truths I've learned is that our intuition is a muscle we cannot take for granted: it is a muscle we must use for it to become strong, for it to become the dominant way in which we move through this world.

I am grateful to the women who came before me, my

mother especially, and the women who worked along-side me, and all that we have learned from each other and together. Without them, and without that first pit in my stomach that I decided to follow when I was just seventeen, I may never have left home, or traveled the world over, or stood on the front lines of history, forever changed by the power of listening to it all.

# I Am Not Lost, I'm Looking

*By Emily Wells*
*Composer*

I've just read something. It took my breath away. Two friends trying to free another friend in his death through dancing. A waltz set to Tomaso Albinoni's "Adagio in G minor," all awkward limbs at first, she a bit more graceful, he made of rubber and grief, until finally moving away from one another they are floating, embodied. I move to the piano where there is no beginning. I am already in the middle, surrendered to sightlessness, only images from the story I've read, and yellow grasses moving in a Texas summer, and smoke billowing out of an old brick factory in bitter winter from the safety of my warm car, and feet on the red bricks that make a street in the West Village on New Year's Eve, kissing in that street, knowing the year has changed by the hollering from bars and rooftops nearby. Then nothing, two keys pressed down on the piano to form a beginning, then another two keys, the second chord, a path to a song.

Remembering the story now, I can think only of their

limbs, heads bowed; my own body can't enter the frame just yet. I need more melody, then the crush of more memory which also feels like seeing the future: disease in the body of a friend; my dog lost in dark woods; a song gone viral written by a teenager, he and his pals in a bedroom in the suburbs, cigarette smoke out the window. I am them, and they are me. Reading the story of the two friends has led me to myself. With the infusion of melody and a chord progression opens my experiences of the natural world. There are places I've been that are moving and still at once: a spring in Iceland, hot meeting cold so that fragile human skin can enter; a man-made lake in the desert turned pink at sunset, cold air rushing up from the brush against your legs at dusk making everything breathe and say *You're alive, you're alive*; a moss-covered room in the middle of the forest so dense and green you could bounce upon its floor like a child on a trampoline; an estuary at a California beach, the river and the ocean rolling against one another like two dogs at play, where I baptized myself in winter, not for forgiveness but for joy; an ancient birch along a trail, the name Elijah carved into its elephant side. These are the places I've been. There are others, not one a copy of another. They resemble music and are like melodies, eternal and static, set down and moving at once.

That day at the piano, with the story of the two friends in my mind, and these secret moving places in my throat, and my own body at hand, with little scraps of literature, magazine articles I half read, a conversation tipsy and passionate in a bar with the winter outside, Kiki Smith's bronze sculpture *Tied to Her Nature*, and everything I've ever wanted and lost, is the beginning of a song. I am at once helpless and at the helm, careening with purpose.

My grandma, a preacher's wife, once dreamed of a house with many rooms catching flame and burning to the ground. The next morning's news revealed a motel fire, just down the road, ash and charred sheets, people in their pajamas standing out on the asphalt. This anecdote was offered up as evidence of her clairvoyance, a thing that gave her a little extra sparkle, set her apart from the rest of the Philistines. Deeply practical and dramatically religious, she was a mix unique to a midcentury American preacher's wife, so pious, so full of gossip and critique, singing full throttle every Sunday morning, the resident soprano. Intuition, clairvoyance, and intelligence were attributed to God, though they were valued as an individual's possessions and cast, not diminutively, as feminine. My mom is even more practical, more analytical, and doesn't tend to entertain a world nor time outside of this one, except heaven. Though extraordinarily capable of awe and curiosity, she did not take on my grandma's claim to clairvoyance, nor was it encouraged of me. But music was. Endless hours of violin practice, choirs, piano, listening, my father in the dining room doing his scales on the French horn. These, all the tools I have been given to know myself and, just maybe, the future.

Not all songs happen the same way, but they all evoke the same hot, breathless feeling, rendering me unsettled until they are complete. If I'm unable to finish the song in a single sitting it becomes my invisible pet, warming my lap wherever I go, on my lips slipping ideas into a conversation to test them out, to look for expansion. I become especially selective about what I read or watch or listen to when a song is brewing. My songs can be thin-skinned, porous, and as influenceable as a teenager at youth group. One moment they'll be in the throes of salvation, the next, smoking a Winston in a patch of woods at the back of the church parking lot. As their guardian, I must remain agnostic and in control of these unsupervised moments away from an instrument, a studio, and/or a recording device. When I do get back in the room with them, I record everything, often crudely, into my voice memos. Songwriting, like intuition, is instinctual, but its memory is far from ironclad. Because the experience of it is so total—of the body, mind, and spirit—you believe it will not leave you under any circumstance, that you will remember every subtlety, every gray and blue, all images coalescing, all harmonies unbroken. And of course the melody will never—*gasp*—leave! But there are hundreds of recorded hours of me pawing around for a song that prove otherwise: a sample made from layers of violin and voice looping unselfconsciously; superfluous lyrics undressing until they become themselves, hung on melodies which open and close like seagrass. Most of these recordings go unlistened to but are made as a safety hatch in my trapdoors of wandering through ideas, melodies, structure, image, and lyric.

Songwriting, like intuition, is something that can be honed and practiced. It enjoys, but does not require, skill. It's not a thing that can be perfected, even though there are plenty of examples of the so-called perfect song. Each experience of writing a song, while familiar, is unique, and the moment it isn't, you know you're walking around in prefab architecture, and you'd best get out before the ceiling caves in. Making a record is similar but heavier-handed because you are drawing nuance out of a delicate form with blunt objects. Blunt because you are making *an object*, you are placing matter into the world where only imagination previously existed. You are translating. You are wandering into thickets of association, language, color, genre, and line that give your song immovable edges. You want to say to the listener, "I promise this thing is still alive. If it is moving in you, it will always have wings, or legs at least." Translation, like songwriting, is an act of love, but it is a delicate form. The French poet Stéphane Mallarmé said, "The imperfection of languages consists in their plurality, the supreme one is lacking." Music may be universal, but recordings of music are languages, and likewise translatable, malleable, plastic as the brain. This is why making a good one, or at least good enough to call it finished, is so difficult. Writing a song often feels lucid, instinctual, physical, more animal, while recording a song—and in particular, mixing one—requires choices and instincts that feel more human. Where in composition there are the basic tenets of structure, melody, and (sometimes) lyric, with recording enters style, instrumentation, technology, musicians, recording technique, methodology, gear...the list goes on and on. In short, you are faced with possibilities which can feel both limitless and confining. Maybe what makes the whole ordeal feel more permanent, requiring rapt attention, is that you are placing an object into the realm of time and giving it the potential to be either remembered or forgotten.

During the mixing of my last record, each song was telling me it was finished through two criteria: one, it sounded as though we were listening to The Record, and two, it felt as if it was waving goodbye. As each potential final print began—the one that would be mastered and pressed on vinyl and streamed on the internet—I would set a barometer in myself, an oracle listening, listening for the truth of it. When it wasn't right, I felt itchy, distracted. I thought of something mundane, a smoothie. It was without magic. "Stop," I'd say, hitting the space bar, turning to Chris, the mixing engineer, and Sam, my partner, who was there to lend what we call her *pedestrian ears* to the final stage of the process. We'd all sigh after holding our breaths, jumping in for all the ways we knew it wasn't *it*. When it was *it*, I'd sometimes choke up a little, silently with hot eyes, my back turned to the others, knowing it was the last time I'd be near the song in this way ever again. Or I'd go back into the memory of the song's making: a run I took the day I finished it, clapping my hands against my legs, finding the rhythm of the lyric under my breath and against my skin, the lone pine tree tall and dignified in the overgrown golf course. In these moments of knowing I'd often get very warm and still, breathing like a dog asleep, every layer a whole.

When I was seventeen a major label, Epic Records, got ahold of a recording I'd made in a damp basement studio. The A&R, or talent scout, who was a VP, a woman who I imagine was in her late thirties and who seemed to me impossibly worldly and impossibly adult, flew to Indianapolis to watch me perform a show arranged for her arrival in a chatty dinner venue. I played my acoustic guitar and sang my earnest songs, trying not to look at her table which seemed lit from a different source than the rest of the restaurant. She was generous, didn't seem fazed by the amateur setting or performer. My newly acquired manager, a former punk rocker à la CBGB, a Brown University dropout, and a proselytizer of his own sobriety was hyper with possibility. The two of them saw that unholiest of qualities gleaming from my seventeen-year-old chest: potential. And so began a two-year game of cat and mouse, the roles ever revolving between A&R and me, the young artist. They gave me money, a *development deal* of ten thousand dollars. I thought I'd be rich forever. I abandoned my invitation to the School of the Art Institute of Chicago and went to New York, Los Angeles, Nashville, Martha's Vineyard, wrote mostly with men at least twice my age in studios amid gear that shimmered and blinked and spun. We ordered takeout. I asked lots of questions about how everything worked. We tried, industriously, to write songs, but they were mediocre at best, impressions, impostors, obvious thieves. They were without magic. "She's like Billie Holiday with beats," the A&R said. I knew intrinsically how wrong this was; I cringed, understanding later in life just how gross and wrong that statement truly was. "She's like Norah Jones, but cool." Also cringe—deep, deep cringe. "They'll be writing books about you," the postpunk manager said. I knew in my elastic bones that if I took this chance to try and say things I didn't yet know how to say, with the giant gears of a major label machine making the whole thing public, I would quickly be rendered mute. I would lose my chance at a future self who *did* know how to speak and make and learn. Fame was a death mask. The closer I got to the machine, the hotter it felt, a refinery that would remake me. So I walked. I ran amok, wandered about for a time, turning my back on the A&R and manager alike, a definitive *no* resounding like a door slammed in a dark stairwell. The decision to do so wasn't an easy one, my young identity still forming and already becoming attached to the life I was being promised and others' perception of me as some kind of prodigy. But prodigies are often in danger of becoming underdeveloped, perpetually precocious adults, and I was crossing that threshold known as adulthood, where prodigies become extinct and decidedly less interesting just for the sake of themselves. I too recognized something akin to potential gleaming from somewhere inside me, but it was shaped more like a lifetime, and its development required the holiest of qualities: privacy and time. While logic, reason, stubborn ideology, and the history of young artists supernova-ing their way into oblivion were certainly present in my process of leaving the record deal on the table, it was my intuition that moved in me to protect my creative life, both present and future. I eventually made a home in Los Angeles, built a tiny studio in an overstuffed garage surrounded by boxes and blankets, a fire trap, I'm sure. There, with the lights off, less dangerous, I learned how to listen in the dark.

Songwriting, like intuition, is not hapless. Its beginnings are often born some place other than my own blazing heart.

The myth of the blazing heart can get the heart-haver in trouble. I have learned that the place to look is not always inside, that much of what I'm looking for is contained in a book or some other record of human experience, often called art. If I'm stuck in my process of making, I read. I look. The two friends dancing in that story which overtook me were the artist and writer David Wojnarowicz and the artist Kiki Smith. They were grieving the death of their friend, the photographer Peter Hujar on the night of his memorial. David wrote about it in his diaries from 1987, later published in the book, *In the Shadow of the American Dream: The Diaries of David Wojnarowicz*. The song I wrote, "Come On Kiki," that arrived in the aftermath of its reading, doesn't attempt to tell their story—nor even to fully understand it—but reading it led me to my own body, my own story, my own knowing or unknowing. It set in me new rhythms and registers, made my voice reach upward. "Oh, hi there, Kate Bush," it said. On some days I might call this habit of reading and reacting *research*. On other days it is simply a process, a way to access myself by entering other people's worlds through their work. I spent an entire summer nursing Mary Ruefle's *Madness, Rack, and Honey* while writing an album called *This World Is Too _____ For You*, whose title came into my mind while lying on a giant beanbag at the New Museum's Pipilotti Rist exhibition in New York.

When I'm not still enough to read, I run or walk the dog. I go to the woods or a river; for a long stint it was the Hudson. I marvel at the American sycamores, the tulip poplars, the light. I reach for awe. I wear myself out. I'm whistling under my breath. I call a friend when I'm desperate, when I'm certain there are no answers to be had. In a bar at the end of the night we find them, the answers. I forget them in the morning. So I go back to the studio, and I read. All the while I am rendering in the background. I catch the eye of a stranger on the train or while crossing the street. It means so much. I read. I write something down, a long scrawl of a something, and hours or days later, I extract two phrases which become ornamental or structural. I'm not sure which just yet. Either way, they are essential. I am not lost, I'm looking. I make peace with the rarity of finding, of its illusion. I can never make peace with this. I read. I check my phone, fallible, distractible, get snagged on the news or jealousies or wit. Sometimes there's something in there for me, more often not.[11] I find imaginary friends, most of them dead but alive through their work. I can hear the crash of waves nearby in Derek Jarman's garden. I am lying under the stars on a railroad track next to Bill T. Jones, but it's a private moment, so neither of us is aware of the other. I am listening as Anna Akhmatova whispers her husband's poems in ears, as told by Joseph Brodsky. Hannah Arendt reminds me I'm more mortal than the fox I see on my daily walk to the woods. These people and the stories they've left give me access to my own imagination, a sibling of my intuition.

It has been twenty years since my dance with the devil— the major label—and I have my own humming luminous

---

11  Except that one time when Twitter leads me to an article about a new invention which makes boulder-sized blocks of ice in the desert. I think its purpose is irrigation. I invent a song from this image. It begins, *Can't make ice in the desert, / can't fool the heavens.*

studio, a collection of records which bear my name, and a small team of adults who count my songs and their reception as part of their job. I have lived at times in service of song, at times in service of self. The former always leaves me more whole, more animal, less mortal. It teaches me that curiosity, intuition's other sibling, is life's most fertile gift, and that making songs, making art, can be an expression of that curiosity. To be in service of... "This can be a lifestyle," says the preacher's granddaughter. To be in service of a song is to serve the listener, even if you are the only one with an ear to the door. I wonder if this is why I was always drawn to the Psalms and Proverbs I grew up with. Psalms so that I would look around the natural world and say, *Yes, this is right, this is dazzling*. Proverbs which say, *Show me how to be this good*.

Whenever I finish making a record, there is a period of time when I start to walk backward, slowly soft-shoeing away from it, trying not to blink, until it is lost to the horizon and I can finally turn around and start running full speed toward some other new place. I tend to forget this process, an amnesiac for the pain of departure. But it's for the best. If I remembered this ungodly wrenching, I'd never make another record again. You see, each time it's gonna be different this time. And each time, it is.

# In Conversation and Friendship: A Dialogue on Navigating Intuition

*America Ferrera and Amber Tamblyn*

Intuition is not just something we possess individually, it is something to be shared. The actress and director America Ferrera and I met in the summer of 2004 when we first worked together on the beloved film, *The Sisterhood of the Traveling Pants*, and we have remained close ever since. We have seen each other through some of life's biggest challenges, celebrations, and mournings. We have danced together on dance floors until 5:00 a.m. and built political movements and vacationed with each other's families. We've given each other some of the best advice and some of the worst hangovers, some of the most cherished pep talks and head checks. We've been to each other's weddings, held each other's newborn babies, held each other while we cried, while we screamed out with joy. We've spent at least five Christmases together, eight New Year's Eves, and three out of the four presidential election nights since we could vote. (On that fourth one, we FaceTimed.)

I asked America to join me one cold winter morning in my kitchen in Brooklyn to talk about what intuition means to her and how she's come to practice and use it in her everyday life. Together, as old friends will often do, we dove in deep to talk about everything intuition related, from how it manifests in our bodies and comes to fruition in our careers, how to heal old traumas of self-doubt and forge new and healthier bonds with our children, and, of course, Beyoncé. Always Beyoncé.

**Brooklyn, New York, 2021**

**Amber Tamblyn:** When you hear the word *intuition*, what comes up for you?

**America Ferrera:** When I hear that word *intuition*, for me it means a deeper knowing about something your body has absorbed before your brain can give it a definition. It's a feeling in my gut, a feeling about what's right for me, or not right for me, or even just something that I can't quite define for myself yet, something that needs the space and time to be revealed.

**AT:** So, intuition is not just something we use to tell us what the right answer is, it's also something we can follow to tell us what the wrong answer is, or even help us understand when we're not sure.

**AF:** Yes. I think there's a lot of power in saying you don't have a *yes* or a *no* yet, that your gut still needs time to process or consider what it has received—it needs a little more time for you to take things in.

**AT:** Intuition is not just what gives you the answers, but what makes you sit longer with the questions.

**AF:** Yeah, and to not be afraid of the discomfort that might rise up from that. For me, a really big part of my maturing, of my growing up and stepping into positions of leadership—both in my professional life but also with regard to my political advocacy work—is about the trust I've built with my intuition, and not always having to explain that trust, or that intuition, to others.

**AT:** Tell me more about that trust, that knowing in your body. When you first feel it, is it just in your body, or does it also live in your mind? Like, does it ever present as a thought first? When you know something is off?

**AF:** It definitely doesn't start in my mind.

**AT**: Can you try and articulate where, exactly, it presents itself? Like, if I was a doctor and was asking you where the pain was, in your body—

**AF:** When it's happening, when my intuition is kicking in, it lives in this space between my gut and my heart. Like, where your solar plexus is.

**AT:** This makes sense. The solar plexus is where the largest network of nerves in the body meet up and cross paths. It's like the Times Square subway station of our bodies. You've got the Adrenal Line! Kidney Line! Liver Line! Stomach Line! Aorta Line! So many nerve lines passing through one area.

**AF:** Exactly! It's no wonder they call it *solar*, because it really does feel like the sun inside you that sheds light on everything else.

**AT:** You're the sun inside me, America.

**AF:** Be quiet. I'm talking.

**AT:** Sorry. Go on.

**AF:** So, the gut–heart connection. When something feels wrong, whether that's with my family, or on a business call, or something in my activist life, I try to tune in to what it feels like in my body, and see if there's a holding in that space where the information is being processed. That part of me literally *holds* itself. When something's happening that doesn't feel aligned to me, there's a holding, like an attention my body is asking for, like a child pulling on her mom's shirt to pay attention to her. It's almost like a protective shutting down.

**AT**: That's the rope pulling you.

**AF:** Yes, that's the rope pulling me. And when things feel right, even if they're really hard, like having to tell someone you don't want to work with them anymore, or passing on an offer for a project that everyone says you should do, or pulling away from an old friendship that no longer serves me—

**AT:** This feels like a really harsh way to tell Beyoncé that you're breaking up with her—

**AF:** Beyoncé *is* my solar plexus, I would *never*.

**AT:** Cool, as long as I'm still the sun inside you.

**AF:** My children are the sun inside me, Amber. You can be, like, a ray or two.

**AT:** I would have literally settled for a flare.

**AF:** When something feels right, there's a softness I feel in my body, a natural and comfortable flow. There's no shutting down, whether that's a person I'm with, a scenario I'm walking into, or the way that I'm behaving in a relationship or with my child. The rope is still pulling, but this time, going with it is easy and feels very right.

**AT:** Let's talk about what it takes to get to this place in our lives where we better understand our intuition. I'm not sure I'm completely there—in the knowing—and I'm almost forty years old. I don't mind it, that I'm still open to the possibility that my relationship to my intuition and what feels right or wrong is still being defined. I've definitely come a very long way since my childhood, as have you. From the fifteen years we've known each other—

**AF:** Girl, it's been almost twenty—

**AT:** Almost twenty years! From the almost twenty years we've known each other, we've seen each other go through so much. *So. Much.* Death, marriage, failure, success, children, revolutionary political movements, crises both existential and literal. We've seen each other through all of it. And we've both worked really hard to get here, pushing past things that have terrified us, hurt us, held us back, challenged us. To get to this place where we can really hear what our intuition is telling us, about our physical health, mental health, emotional health, and psychological health.

**AF:** Very true.

**AT:** We both carried a lot of anxiety as kids—pretty bad anxiety—and a sense of feeling nervous about outcomes. While we had very different upbringings, we were still both child actresses in an era where girls and women were treated differently than they are today, and of course yours was compounded even further by being a woman of color. You've come such a long way from that girl you once were. Do you remember if you had any connection to your gut when you were younger, in the way that you do now? Maybe you were that in tune with yourself then, but you couldn't articulate it at the time? Or do you think it's a thing you found later on in your life?

AF: I've always been a very sensitive and tapped-in person, especially as a child. From as young as I can remember, I was always feeling whatever unspoken dynamics were happening in the room. I've always had a heightened radar for that. I think most children do. But I didn't know to trust my own feelings, and I certainly didn't know what to do with those feelings once they were acknowledged in my body, when and if they were trusted. For instance, several years ago, when I was learning about my intuition and how to harness it, I spent a whole year training for my very first triathlon. It was a really, really, really big deal for me—

AT: Right, I remember this—

AF: Because of all of the stories that I have about my body. I had this whole story about this car accident I was in when I was a teenager, and how I hurt my shoulder, and that hurt extended out to other parts of my body, and in a way, became a crutch for me—a reason not to deal with the other traumas of my body. It was true, I was in an accident, and the pain was real, but the story about the origin of the pain was not.

AT: What do you mean?

AF: Yes, I had injured myself in a car accident, but no, it was not and could not be the source of all the pain I was feeling. Because when I really thought about it, when I began to ask questions of myself, the pain actually began way before that car accident; it began somewhere in my childhood. The car accident just brought attention to it. And by the time I was twenty-five years old, I was in crippling pain all over. I told myself my neck pain and back pain were chronic and would always be there. That I'd never be able to do anything athletic, I'm just not built that way, that this kind of suffering is just normal. The story I've told myself about that pain is how I've been able to feel disconnected from my body's power, from its usefulness as a tool beyond something I just happened to inhabit. I had to actively transform my relationship to my body to change the story of what my body could mean to me.

**AT:** That is so powerful. So, you understood that to connect on a deeper level with your gut, with your intuition, you first had to not just heal your body but heal the story your body had been telling you your entire life, that it couldn't be trusted because it was forever injured.

**AF:** Exactly. My relationship to my body also changed my emotional life. I realized it was all one and the same. There was no cause and effect. It was like you had to deal with both at the same time because that's where emotion lives. I realized that everything I've ever experienced, every emotion I've ever had, every trauma, every joy, every memory has happened in this one vessel. This, right here, is where it all lies. Training for that triathlon was so confronting because it made me think about all the dissociating I have done—I have had to do to protect myself—since I was young. Because the truth is, it always felt uncomfortable to be in my body.

**AT:** How so?

**AF:** There were so many ridiculous expectations placed on women's and girl's bodies back then, when we were growing up, and under the public eye, no less. It was the era of Britney Spears, of tween movies starring rail-thin actresses, none of whom were of color. This is why the first film I made at seventeen years old, *Real Women Have Curves*, was so revolutionary—because those kinds of bodies and stories just did not exist on-screen. But the existence of that film felt like an anomaly, not a normality. There were so many ridiculous standards about what was the right way to look or the right way to be, and I was constantly being told I was none of those things, and so that's the story my body latched on to. Living in my body—*feeling* in my body *without* anxiety—was not something I did or knew how to do. I had been taught from such a young age that so much about my body was not right, from the way that I looked to the way that I felt. But how can you trust something—a body that houses your intuition—when you've been told your entire life it is wrong?

**AT:** So you literally had to start from scratch with your body. You had to start over and teach it a new story.

**AF:** Yes. I distinctly remember the moment: I was actually at your house upstate, on your big trampoline. I jumped two times on the trampoline and started crying because my neck and back hurt so badly. I was twenty-five years old! I was otherwise in good health and had no reason to feel like this. I knew right then and there I didn't want to spend the rest of my life feeling this way. And that's when I really started to deal with the physical pain and how much it was linked to so much emotional pain, for so many years and for so many reasons. And they fed into each other. How could they not? This was the story! *My* story. My emotional pain causes trauma, and then—

**AT:** The trauma causes the emotional pain.

**AF:** Yes, that was step one for me, to teach my body a new story so that it would stop telling the one about how broken and wrong it was. And I did get there. I started to go through this healing, this transformation after that experience on the trampoline, in my late twenties. I started asking myself more questions. Is this pain still real? What does it say about me that I'm always in pain and am not suffering from a disease or an underlying condition? That I have no real reason to be so? I started to seek out healers who would help me answer these questions. I started to work with an osteopath and a physical therapist, and I did traditional psychotherapy for years, sometimes even a few times a week. I did a lot of work on myself to change my story and my relationship to my body, until I finally got to a place in my thirties where I could actually do an entire marathon and not feel broken after it. Once I did that work, and strengthened my body, and found a new relationship to it, then I could start to listen to it. To trust it when it was telling me something.

**AT:** I feel like your relationship to your intuition is really strong—

**AF:** Yes, it is, and I can feel it very presently in my body—

**AT:** And acutely—

**AF:** Yeah, literally right here between my ribs.

**AT:** You know that expression *shoot from the hip*? I feel like you shoot from the gut. That's who you are. Do you ever second-guess that shot?

**AF:** Yes, of course I do. That's the other part of intuition I mentioned—the part of yourself that is still learning, that maybe doesn't have the answer yet, or is unsure if what you're feeling is your intuition or past traumas manifesting somehow and taking over in the moment. I am very cognizant of that.

**AT:** This describes something that I think a lot of women face: a pendulum swing of second-guessing yourself, of wondering if what you are feeling is the motivation of your new story or your old story—of old traumas or new relationships to the self.

**AF:** Exactly. It isn't until you are fully connected to your body that you can sense when that old story is trying to take over and you can instead push past it. This is how you flex your intuitive muscle.

**AT:** Tell me more about that muscle.

**AF:** I think that our intuition is like a muscle, and if you don't use it, it atrophies. If you don't use it or don't even know how to identify it, then you also don't even know that you have intuition or it exists to begin with.

**AT:** Like my abs.

**AF:** Like your abs. And the way that you get stronger in your intuition is by using it, working it out. By having the courage to act on your intuition, to listen, to actually pay attention to and be in constant consultation with it.

**AT:** I am thinking about that scene in the finale of season three of *Succession* when Gerri looks a groveling Roman dead in the eye after he begs her to save his legacy, and she softly says, "It doesn't serve my interests. How does it serve my interests?" So cutthroat. So good.

**AF:** And we have to let our intuition ask those cutthroat questions! We have to let our intuition be *selfish*. Because if our intuition is speaking to us and we just choose to ignore, ignore, ignore, it goes away, or it gets silenced, it gets very dull. You have to let it ask the outside world how your interests are being served, even if that makes you incredibly uncomfortable or terrified or even disliked. And then you have to act on what that intuition is telling you. It could be easy, or it could be really hard, like telling your friend how that thing they said or did made you feel—

**AT:** I apologize for that, by the way.

**AF:** How does the way you cooked me those eggs serve my interests, Amber? It doesn't serve my interests.

**AT:** What's it like to have a number one best friend like me, and how do the other numbers feel about it? It must be very hard for them.

**AF:** It is *so* hard. And yes, intuition is a muscle that you must flex even when you don't want to. I've gotten stronger and been able to pinpoint what I feel and how I feel it. I know in the moment, when I get that feeling in my gut, a holding or a flowing, either way I know what's right for me, and yes, maybe it's going to be uncomfortable to act on it, but I'm going to do it. And then once I've done it, everything feels so much better and so much more aligned, like a good workout.

**AT:** You've worked out that intuitive muscle!

**AF:** Yep! And after you do it one time—even just once— you now know about that muscle and how to get it to work for you. That it is there to serve you. You learn that listening to your intuition, even if it's hard, will always end in a better outcome. It's like, Oh, what's that feeling? Oh, I'm getting a message from myself about something that's not working for me. Am I going to ignore that message? Am I going to live with that message? Am I going to fester in that message? Or am I just going to listen to it? Act on it? And when you act on it, it may not always be 100 percent right, but at least you're headed in that direction. You're stretching and strengthening that muscle.

**AT:** Can you tell readers a little bit more about what working on that muscle looked like, to get you where you are today? What are some of the practices you've done to strengthen it?

**AF:** I guess setting up boundaries in my life with relationships and family members that just don't serve me. Setting up those boundaries, especially with family, was the scariest thing I've ever done. I could cry right now thinking about it. There are relationships I've had to say goodbye to, had to disconnect from, had to pull away from for my own mental health. Doing this, however difficult, changed everything for me. It gave me the permission and the safe space to decide what is the right environment for me to grow in, to feel good in, and then take responsibility for that environment. Setting up those family boundaries was very, very difficult, but it allowed me to begin my journey toward healing.

I've also worked on my intuition muscle through creative dream work that I've been doing now with my creative coach for fourteen years. All of this work I've been doing—for the body and the story and the creative journey—has allowed me to create a path to have full faith in what my gut wants me to understand. The active practice, of hearing it, of listening to it, and then acting on it, is the most important part, for any of us. I have the capacity to tap into something that feels more supportive and held and aligned with what's good for me and what I need than anything that I can rationalize in my brain.

**AT:** Tell me more about how the creative dream work fits into all of this, your work to heal trauma and forge this new relationship to your intuition.

**AF:** So we've talked about the body, we've talked a bit about our brains and our emotions—

**AT:** Also can I just say, people reading this don't realize that this kind of conversation is just, like, a casual Wednesday for us.

**AF:** Oh, for sure. I don't know how to keep my deep, dark feelings to myself.

**AT:** Totally. I don't fuck with you unless you fuck with *talking about your emotions*.

**AF:** Exactly.

**AT:** "Hey, America, want to meet up for some coffee and talk about our most secret worst fears and desires?"

**AF:** "Totes! Right after you tell me about the generational trauma passed down to you through your matriarchal line."

**AT:** Ha! So real.

**AF:** So yeah—there's the work of the body, there's the work of the mind, therapy and all that. And then there's also our subconscious dream life. I think about the images that come to me in my dreams and how important it is to really value them.

**AT:** Your dream life is so deeply connected to your subconscious, which is an echo of your intuition. To know that voice is to know what you want for your life and for your art.

**AF:** Yes! I can't think of anything more stressful, as an actress, as a director, as an artist, than having to decide my work based on what I think other people want. What *I'm* dreaming up is valuable and worthy of my time and my creative energy and my expression. To me, not only is that incredibly fulfilling personal work, it's also the only work I know how to do. I can't sit here and say that the story that's going to sell is more important than the story that needs to be told. The personal, the emotional, the physical, the creative, it all feels to me like it is part of the same wellspring. And the more you can be in touch with all of that, the better. Some people do it by meditating, some people do it by running, some people do it by cooking. I mean, when do you get to sit with your own impulses and express yourself from that place?

**AT:** We don't, really. Maybe some of us do, as children, if we're lucky to grow up in an environment that's conducive to that. As adults, especially as women, we are conditioned to get rid of any part of us that is wild—any part that is dangerous, disagreeable, or even feral; unkempt and uncontrollable. As children, we're so in tune with those parts of ourselves, getting lost in the beautiful wilderness of our imaginations and wherever they might take us. We are radical as children, and the wellspring is flourishing.

**AF:** Yes, and then it is all trained out of us by polite society, which doesn't want to hear what that wild part of us has to say anymore. As a child, I knew I wanted to act. The first time I saw my sister [act], I was in kindergarten, five years old. My sister was in her fifth-grade play. She was a monkey in *The Wizard of Oz*. And I sat in the audience and burned with rage. Not jealousy, but just, the rage of knowing that's what I should be doing, right there on that stage. But the truth is, there's only one map that anyone offers us to get there as actors. It says *This is what an actor is. This is what an actor looks like. This is what an actor sounds like. This is the only path of an actor.* And so you learn how to meet all of those expectations and you hit all of those marks. And that's what I did, because that's all I knew how to do at the time.

**AT:** Because for you, for a while, success meant being really good at just this one thing, right? Not being seen as someone who contains multitudes of talent, a multi-hyphenate with many different talents to be proud of. You only worked to be acknowledged for this one thing—acting—and you excelled in it, no matter the personal or existential cost.

**AF:** Yes, because to be really good at this one thing, and to be validated for being really good at this one thing, that would mean I made the dream come true. That would mean I had not failed that little girl inside me. And everything outside of that was just other parts of me that were not as important, meaningful, or valuable as the thing that I had decided as a child I needed to be successful at. The dream work I have been doing for over a decade has so much to do with letting go of that picture—of mourning that dream so that I could open space for other ones to have just as much meaning in my life.

**AT:** What kind of other dreams?

**AF:** The dream of becoming a director and producer, of not just acting in my own work but actively creating it. Of having the space to have both children and a career in my life, and a good partner to live alongside and do all these things with. And so far, I have been able to do all these things. Maybe not all in perfect balance, but I know now how to truly value my own judgment and to do what feels right to me, and not what feels right to everyone else. For most of my life, I had been doing the latter. But I do feel like I still struggle in a lot of ways with following my gut when that might disappoint other people, or feel like an inconvenience to them. That is, for me, the work I am still doing.

**AT:** Can you give me an example of what that might look like in your life?

**AF:** Years ago, when I was going through this shift of listening to my body and my gut, there was a project I was asked to do as an actress, and I said yes to it, but I told them I also wanted to be a producer because I knew I had a lot to creatively give behind the camera. They weren't so sure about it at first and pushed back, because when an actress asks for that in their contract, it's assumed that it's a vanity credit, a token title to have in lieu of more money. But I stood by what I felt and knew that I needed to be a part of the decision-making process. They eventually agreed to it. But once I got on set, I was so terrified to use that power.

I was so afraid that the other producers would see me as difficult, or a fraud, or that what I would be bringing to the table would be perceived as not being about the bigger picture of making this project the best it could be. And even though I knew where I was coming from, and knew that my feelings and my thoughts and my notes were about being in service of the greater good, I was so afraid that I would just end up fulfilling their projection of who I was. I would find myself in my trailer crying because I wanted to have a conversation about something I felt could use some work in the script, but I was so afraid that if I did, I'd somehow be proving them right.

**AT:** There's that pendulum swing of second-guessing again.

**AF:** Yes. And it devastated me and confused me. I sat there in my trailer crying and thinking, Why can't I do this? Have a simple conversation as the producer I now am? I fought to have this power, I fought to be a part of this conversation, and now I'm afraid to have it. What am I afraid of? Am I afraid they'll say, no? No, I can hear a no. Am I afraid I won't know what to say? No, I know what to say. I'm an articulate person, I have strong opinions and useful ideas about how to make this script stronger. So what is it? And when it came down to it, I was afraid that they wouldn't like me. That using my power, that I had fought so hard to get, would contradict me being a likable person.

**AT:** And how did that revelation make you feel? Did it change anything?

**AF:** I was shocked by how simple that was and how powerful it was at holding me back. There are times where we can ask for what we want and feel fine about that and stand up for ourselves. But then you turn around and there's the challenge all over again. Like, okay, well now I have this power, but how do I use the power? And that was a really big one for me. Once I saw it—this need to be liked over being heard—I knew I had to push through it.

**AT:** How do you push through it?

**AF:** I would say to myself, Okay, America, we're all adults so let's have an adult conversation. And if they hypothetically say no, then you go from there, but it's okay to have the conversation. I acknowledged that what was standing in the way of me using my intuition was my fear of how it would reflect back on me. I also didn't punish myself for needing people to like me—needing people to like me has served me in a lot of ways as someone who started out as a poor, brown woman in this world and in the entertainment industry. That's a really useful weapon to know how to use, to make people like you, and to be pleasant enough, and not threatening enough, so that people *want* to include you in the conversation.

**AT:** So just identifying the underlying fear was enough to help you make sense of it so you could recognize it again, if and when it happens, and push through it?

**AF:** Yes, it was about identifying the fear and listening to the voice that talked me through it. And then the next time it would come up, I would just remember, Oh right, that's what that is. There's that feeling again. Okay. I'm going to acknowledge it, and even if my literal voice is shaking and I'm feeling nervous, I'm going to speak. I'm going to follow my intuition in this moment. I'm going to flex this muscle.

**AT:** It sounds like being able to name the fear, to name why it's there, what it is, really helps you to be able to put one foot in front of the other and keep moving forward, no matter how hard the hike.

**AF:** Yes, and that, right there, is the actual practice of it. You can't wait to act when there is no fear, when something is easy or when it won't affect someone else.

**AT:** We learn that in childhood—to shut down our emotional and creative lives in order to become functioning, easy-going members of society.

**AF:** Yeah. The way I deal with my fear is to treat it like I'm its parent. "I see you, I know you're scared, you can feel that way, but we're still going to speak up now, okay?" And the fear inside you might kick and scream and say *No, no, no.* But it's allowed to! You're allowed to be scared!

**AT:** You've talked about the child body and the adult body here, and the string of trauma that runs through both of them and how the latter is so informed by the former. I know for me, I had to do so much therapy and work to process my experience as a child actress growing up in Hollywood. What would you say to someone reading this book who isn't part of the entertainment industry? Does this work still apply to them? What would you say to the scared child in them that you had to say to yourself? The one who is not yet ready to trust themselves, or listen to their intuition, because they were told their bodies are wrong, their feelings are wrong, their existence is somehow wrong. How would you enter into the conversation, to begin to show them the way?

**AF:** This is a big and vital question. You know I have two children. And I think about this all the time, because the years, and the money, and the energy, and the heartache that I have spent on undoing all the damaged messaging I took in as a child is heartbreaking. So I would say this to your readers. I want you to know that everything you feel is okay. Everything. How you feel is good enough. And being afraid is definitely very okay. You have the power to be authentically who you are, in spite of your old story, in spite of your fear. I know for me, I have the opportunity to be the kind of parent that makes it so my children don't have to grow up and spend their lives undoing. You can be that parent to yourself, too. To the dreams of your child-self. And when you acknowledge that truth for yourself, your body will give in to you. It will help you find the way. For instance, I would never tell my kids not to be scared. "It's just a loud noise, don't be scared!" I would never say that. I would say, "That scared you, didn't it? I can see that. But you're safe, I got you." Because the fear is real for them, and I don't ever want them to believe that what they feel is wrong. I don't want to set them up for a life like that.

**AT:** Powerful.

**AF:** A tool that my therapist gave me when I was just starting my therapy journey was to imagine myself as a child and to think about how I would talk to that child during moments of crisis.

**AT:** My therapist did something similar. He made me carry around the youngest picture I could find during a moment in which I'm very happy. The picture I found was when I was about three or four years old, and I'm on a rocking horse in my parents' living room, mid-swing, terrified but also screaming with joy.

**AF:** It's so powerful, and doing exercises like this changed everything for me. I remember at some point in my career, singing became a deathly huge fear. I could not sing without my voice shaking. And I was determined—

**AT:** And you're a really good singer! You have such a beautiful Broadway voice!

**AF:** Thank you, friend. And yet, I was so scared to do anything in my career that involved singing. But I was determined to get over it. So I would say yes to all these singing auditions, not because I thought I'd get the job but because I was like, I have to break this fear, and I don't know where it's coming from. And then one day I had an audition for something I actually really did want, but I was so afraid that this fear was going to come in and make it impossible for me to sing well. I remember taking the subway to the audition, and my whole body was shaking. I remember thinking, Maybe I could get hit by a car, just a little bit, and then I won't have to go to this audition—

**AT:** If a car could just run over one of my legs, that would be great—

**AF:** Or just my foot. Anything to not have to go. But I did what my therapist said, and I made myself imagine little nine-year-old America standing outside of that building, wanting to throw up, legs shaking, swamped in fear. And I imagined just holding her hand and saying, "It's okay that you're afraid, you're allowed to be afraid, and you can go in and you can do this, even though you're afraid." I said to myself, Getting this role in this movie doesn't say anything about you, and *not* getting this role in this movie also doesn't say anything about you. And your fear isn't bad, it doesn't make you weak, it just means that you're human. Then, I went in, did the audition, and though my voice was shaking and I was terrified, I did a beautiful job, and the audition went great.

**AT:** Please tell me this was for the movie *From Justin to Kelly* starring Kelly Clarkson.

**AF:** It was, and it should've been called *From Justin to America*, thank you very much.

**AT:** There's still time for a sequel!

**AF:** The point is, this is a tool we can all use to start to get closer to that inner voice—that intuition inside us. What would you say to your child, or your best friend, if they were scared? If they felt these things about themselves? How would you treat them? Would you say, "You're being ridiculous, you're such a coward, you're so weak, get over it, suck it up"? No, you wouldn't. So treat yourself that same way. Because I was not treated that way growing up, I know how that model turned out. My family called me a drama queen anytime I had a big feeling. The way I felt didn't matter. It needed to be suppressed. It needed to be scolded and dismissed. And I was a very sensitive child.

**AT:** A very empathic child.

**AF:** Yeah. And I see the way my son is—I see it in him, he feels *everything*. And I am right there with him, feeling it, acknowledging it, saying, "Wow, that was scary when that happened." Or "Oh, that was exciting when the sirens went by." I am letting him know that I see what he's feeling, and it's okay. I didn't have any of that growing up. I had a family that mostly told me that I was overdramatic and that I was overemotional, and they would laugh at me, point fingers at me. I was ridiculed as a child for these feelings, for my emotions.

When I think about that person who feels so alone and so unseen in their feelings, when they feel like there's no one they can go to, that therapy is not an option, or they don't have friends who will understand, or they don't know what dream work is or how to begin that process, I want those people to know that the teacher is already inside them. That those feelings are information, and really valuable information. What you feel can be used to express who you are, if you listen closely. For me, as a child, I know that acting was my way of expressing. It was a way for me to express feelings that wouldn't be seen as too big. It was a place where all that I am belonged. And for other people, that space might be painting or singing or writing or digging in the dirt.

**AT:** You're saying that because not everybody has people they can reach out to, it's important that we do everything we can to find a safe place to process all the ways in which we feel unseen, and that place can be within us. Practice with yourself, with your fear, be the parent to yourself that you perhaps did not have.

**AF:** Exactly. I was looking at photos of myself as a child the other day, and I thought, God, it fucking sucked to be that kid. And it didn't have to be that way. It really sucked to be that kid. To always feel like something was wrong with me, that my body was wrong, who I was was wrong, what I wanted was wrong, what I felt was wrong. To a lot of adults around me, everything I was or did was never okay, and it was never enough. It's so important to find a space for yourself for some good, solid listening and healing for that child inside you.

**AT:** When you talk about how your body always intuitively knows the answer—the solar plexus (aka the Beyoncé Chakra) and how it holds or how it's soft and open—it feels to me like this is your child-self responding. And while this little girl is here to warn you when something makes you feel like she used to, such as being unheard or not valued, she's also there sometimes to disrupt—to give you a warning signal. To remind you of the old story, the old fear.

**AF:** Yes, and I think knowing that part actually serves a really big purpose. Knowing that those defense mechanisms like fear or shame or anger, while they belong, they belong in their place. They don't belong at the center of our decision-making or at the center of how we act. And the denying of them, or the resentment of them, or the need to have those feelings go away, that's a losing battle, because they won't, especially if you've never acknowledged them in the first place. It's a losing battle to say, Oh well, I'm afraid again, I guess this is just a terrible quality in me and speaks to my character, everyone better just get used to it. No. Instead you can say, Ah, yes, I know that part of me, that's the part that wants to protect me from being ridiculed. She's not wrong. I've needed to protect myself from that. And from the adult perspective, from where I sit, I can actually see that I'm okay, I'm safe. I'm safe to be who I am. I'm safe to speak my mind. And even if I don't like what I hear, I'm strong enough to deal with the response. I can tell myself that feeling those feelings is not going to make me a child again who is laughed at. I don't need to go there ever again. It's like setting out all the little children inside of you who have all these different big feelings and saying, Okay, here's the deal, you're going to be in the back, and you're going to be in your car seat, and you really don't get to drive, and you definitely need a nap. And you can all feel the way you need to feel about these decisions, but that's what we're doing. Period. Just be the parent, and take responsibility for all the babies inside you, and learn to love them, even when they're at their worst. And loving them through it doesn't mean they get to take over.

**AT:** Learn to listen to your body and its story. Reshape

your relationship to your body, because it's the temple for your intuition—for the part of you that has your best interests at heart.

**AF:** Yes. And get therapy of any kind, if you have access to it. Or meditate. Write your dreams down, the ones when you sleep, and the ones you think about during the day. Listen to what they're saying. See how it fits into the bigger picture of your life.

**AT:** Create strong boundaries with people who don't serve you or who have harmed you. Carve out space to create an environment for you to grow safely in.

**AF:** Tell yourself that how you feel is worthy. Being scared is not the end of the road, it's an obstacle you can and will overcome. Go inward and ask yourself if you're afraid, and if you are, tell yourself it's okay. Be the parent to your intuition, to your inner voice. Locate your own personal Beyoncé Chakra and protect it at all costs.

**AT:** I am the sun inside America Ferrera.

**AF:** You are not. But you've definitely been a light in the dark when I needed one.

*Close your eyes and picture a window
centered inside you.*

---

*See it opening.*

---

*Listen.*

*What do you hear?*

# The Road Map, Realized

*By Amber Tamblyn*

From these stories, we have ventured out into a vast land of intuitive inquiry and discovery. We have located the landmarks and land mines of our history, of what women before us have built, demolished, detonated, and birthed. We have wandered through valleys of different experience, rivers of testimony, mountains of observation, dense forests of evidence. We have come to crossroads which mirror our own and read as each choice was made along the way. We recognize all the shared obstacles: the forks in the road, the steep inclines of our learning, the dizzying hills and severe bends which beg us to slow down, look, see, listen.

We have recognized parts of our paths in each of these journeys: a past pain in a current ache, a familiar howl in a future hymn. We have found our sit spots, our quiet spaces, new knowledge from the knowing. We contemplate our reflections, what we see in our mirror. We tune inward, toward what makes us hold, what fills our chests with dread, what trembles in our gut—what thrusts us into action or what brings us to our knees. We do this in order to save lives, to harness what can heal from Earth's bounty. We eat from its dirt like our sorcery's in it. We follow rainbows toward their signs, glean from the faces of clocks what will soon be lost. We sit in a circle, open to the field, dream of earthquakes, of fathers, of fire, of wolves. We parent ourselves in order to better parent our children, our careers, our relationships, our art. We pull wounded stories from our bodies and give them back to their unruly pasts. We get down in the dark of our own quiet, nose pressed against a question, fingers digging deep into its answers. We hold space for all of it. Even when we fear, we doubt, we attempt to distract—we hold space for all of it. We honor the volatility of being human, the difficulty of being Woman.

Here, at the end of this book, something else is being born from its pages. Some new beginning that belongs to you and only you. Yes, *you*. If we have read evidence of each woman's map—how she finds a window within and listens through to what is being intuited—then there is a map for you, too. Let us chart it together, outlining a unique way in, pushing past any resistance, struggle, or deflection used to stop it from happening. Let us let it happen, together. Take all that we have learned from these explorations and build a blueprint to be followed, toward that window inside you that's been waiting, all your life, to be opened. It is your gift, a sacred rite to be realized: what can be ignited when your body and your mind align, allowing your intuition, your inner voice, your knowing, to actualize.

It might take days or even weeks to get there. It can be rough terrain in uncharted territory—mapping a path to your intuitive voice—but one that gets easier with practice and perseverance. You might find yourself starting over and over again, like a pole vaulter propelled toward the bar, until finally, after much practice, you reach the other side. Let us reach the other side, together.

The next time a question is asked of you that requires deep contemplation or a decision must be made under difficult circumstances, follow the map:

*First: Hold.*
Focus on the question. On what you want an answer to.
Pause any quick thought until you can feel
something in your body other than its own living.
Look for signs in your pulse,
in your breathing,
in alternative sensations;
some foreign desire moving or sitting down inside you.

Keep holding.

No one deserves the answer before you do,
and you owe no one a thing.
*You owe no one, anything.*

Don't speak just to appease the silence.
This silence was born for you to hold it.

Once you feel something in your body, see which way it leans.

Does your mind translate a meaning from its tilt?
What is the answer your mind wants to give you?
Before you agree, check back in with your body:
Does the answer from your mind feel correct to your body?

Correctness doesn't mean safety. The answer may not make
you feel safe, at first.
You might want to pull away from what you hear, what
you discover, to recede toward an easier answer. Maybe
your body's way of aligning with your mind's response is
by feeling in complete opposition to it. Maybe your body
feels ill, your throat tightens, your stomach seizes, you feel
revulsion, nervousness, a sense of extreme fragility, a need
to run. Or maybe your body's way of aligning with your
mind's response comes with more ease, making you feel
spun of gold, warm and calm, fluorescent, bright—rich
with possibility.

Either way, you are doing everything just right.
So continue to hold.
Suspend your reaction to this discovered answer for however long it must take. Give this pause your grace, the space
to make you feel whatever needs to be felt to continue.

Whisper to it, out loud now: *You're doing everything just right.*
*I'll wait. I'll wait for you to get here.*

Keep holding.
Let it try and take you away from the answer, make you
cry, fill you with anger or make you numb.

Let it try and distract you with other, shinier, easier out-comes.

Always return to the holding.
*You're doing everything just right. I'll wait. I'll wait for you to get here.*

When the reaction has quieted, has calmed its tantrum, try and separate your fear from its truth;
Split yourself in two: the you that is feeling this reaction, and the you that is in authority. Be a parent to it. A mother to your child. Or big sister to your little one. Be a map to your road, or the woods to your wolf.

Move delicately and with compassion into a state of confrontation with your resistance to this newfound answer. Your resistance may not want to hear it, but it is your job to help it be heard. This is the most valuable relationship you will have in your life, and the more you take care of it, the easier the listening will become.

Speak to it, hold it, listen to it as if it is separate from you, even though it isn't.

What does it say to you?

*I am afraid of this answer because it will destroy the life I've built.*
*Because it will hurt someone I love.*
*Because my children will be affected.*
*Because it will bankrupt me.*

*Because my community will think differently of me.*
*Because I am not good enough.*
*Because I don't deserve it.*
*Because my family will be ashamed of me.*
*Because my peers will laugh at me.*
*Because it's far too much work and will take too much time to achieve.*
*Because I will have to let go of so much that I have worked so hard for.*
*Because I will have to think about what happened to me and I don't want to.*
*Because my mind already told me I couldn't.*
*Because the world around me won't allow it.*
*I won't allow it, for myself.*

Keep holding.

*You're doing everything just right. I'll wait. I'll wait for you to get here.*

Soon there will be an acceptance. Soon there will be a release. Soon what was trying to take you out will give in. It might feel like resignation, or failure, a deep sadness or a grave loss. It might feel like emancipation. It might feel like freedom.

Your body has given you an answer, and while your mind tried at first to dissuade you, you held. You kept holding. You pushed through to the window until you heard what you needed to hear from within. It may not have been easy. You may feel broken or, for the first time in your life, restored.

Either way, you have the answer now—the one reached and born from you and only you. From the collection of your instincts, of your whole life's experiences, of the practice and application of your most vital intuitive voice.

You are doing everything just right. It belongs to you now, this knowing. It is yours to decipher from, newly excavated from the dark, ready for your light.

★ ★ ★ ★ ★

# Acknowledgments

Thank you to the brilliant and generous contributors who made this project everything I ever hoped it would be: Mindy Nettifee, Nicole Apelian, Meredith Talusan, Emily Wells, Jessica Valenti, America Ferrera, Samantha Irby, Jia Tolentino, Huma Abedin, Lidia Yuknavitch, Amy Poehler, Ada Limón, Dara Kass, Congresswoman Ayanna Pressley, and my mom, Bonnie Tamblyn. Your stories, insight, and wisdom brought so much to this book and I'm so honored to have you in its pages.

Extra-special shout-out to Jia Tolentino for giving me the gift of Miami, right when I needed it.

Big love and gratitude for: Ayana Elizabeth Johnson, Ashley C. Ford, Cindi Leive, Meena Harris, and Priya Parker.

This book exists because of my literary agent Anthony Mattero's continual and unwavering belief in my ideas and my work. And this book especially exists because of Laura Brown, its editor and my partner-in-intuition. This isn't our first book together, Laura, and you better believe it's not gonna be our last. Thank you for everything.

Thank you to Team Park Row Books! Heather Connor, Laura Gianino, and Justine Sha in publicity and Amy Jones, Randy Chan, and Rachel Haller in marketing, as well as Lindsey Reeder. Thank you as well to Erika Imranyi, Rachel Reiss, and Margaret Marbury.

Grateful to my teams, who work to bring my wildest

dreams to life: Alla Plotkin and Amanda Pelletier at ID PR for always being in my corner and working so hard on behalf of projects like these. Trinity Ray, Kevin Mills, Ariel Lewiton, Alexa Starry, Ryan Barker, and Mishma Nixon at Tuesday Agency, and Nancy Gates at UTA. Thank you, Aly Sarafa, for your sharp eye, research and assistant work, and Liz Chancey, for your hammers, drills, gardening skills, and so much more.

Many thanks to the institutions and people who aided in the research and exploration for this book: the New York Public Library, Dr. Gerd Gigerenzer, the Carl Jung Institute of New York, the Neurosciences Research Foundation, and the ARDA (Association of Religion Data Archives) at the Library of Congress.

Grateful for those who inspired, supported, and nurtured along the way: Laurel Schmidt, Eliza Clark, Kinga Michalik, Anand Giridharadas, Aviva Yael, Amy Schumer, Mary Katherine Michiels, Ben Foster, April Jones, Samantha Nye, and Stacy Armoogan Bacchus. Thank you to the deer, the wild turkeys, and the eastern white pine trees of Upstate New York.

Thank you to the healers who kept my body and my spirit in shape throughout the writing and research process: Dr. Mary Bayno, Lisa Love, John D'Aguanno, Jun Ichino, Josh Hanson, and Evan F.

Extra-special thank-you, with love and appreciation, for Laura Prepon. Don't make it weird.

And to my family: my husband, David Cross, and Marlow Alice Cross. I love you.

This book is also dedicated to Agneta Falk.

# Endnotes

Simon McCarthy-Jones, Maria Castro Romero, Roseline McCarthy-Jones, Jacqui Dillon, Christine Cooper-Rompato, Kathryn Kieran, Milissa Kaufman, and Lisa Blackman, *Hearing the Unheard: An Interdisciplinary, Mixed Methodology Study of Women's Experiences of Hearing Voices (Auditory Verbal Hallucinations)*, 2015
https://www.frontiersin.org/articles/10.3389/fpsyt.2015.00181/full

Brianna Barkocy, *Madness or Mysticism: An Analysis of the Interpretation of Hearing Voices as Auditory Hallucination or Religious Experience*, 2019
https://epublications.regis.edu/cgi/viewcontent.cgi?article=1933&context=theses

Gerd Gigerenzer, *Homo Heuristicus: Why Biased Minds Make Better Inferences*, Max Planck Institute for Human Development, Max Planck Institute, 2011

Barbara L. Fredrickson and Tomi-Ann Roberts, *Objectification Theory: Toward Understanding Women's Lived Experiences and Mental Health Risks*, 1997
https://www.raggeduniversity.co.uk/wp-content/uploads/2018/04/FredricksonRoberts-ilovepdf-compressed1.pdf

Jonathan W. Marshall, *Performing Neurology: The Dramaturgy of Dr. Jean-Martin Charcot*, Palgrave Macmillan, 2016

Simon McCarthy-Jones, *Hearing Voices: The Histories, Causes and Meanings of Auditory Verbal Hallucinations*, Cambridge University Press, 2013

Erich Neumann, *The Great Mother: An Analysis of the Archetype*, Princeton University Press, 2015

Mary Beard, *Women and Power: A Manifesto*, Liveright, 2017

Rupert Sheldrake, *The Sense of Being Stared At, and Other Unexplained Powers of Human Minds*, Park Street Press, 2011

Katherine May, *Wintering: The Power of Rest and Retreat in Difficult Times*, Riverhead Books, 2020

Malcolm Gladwell, *Blink: The Power of Thinking Without Thinking*, Back Bay Books, 2007

Peter A. Levine, *In an Unspoken Voice: How the Body Releases Trauma and Restores Goodness*, North Atlantic Books, 2017

Gerd Gigerenzer, *Gut Feelings: The Intelligence of the Unconscious*, Tantor, 2007

Carl Jung, *The Collected Works of C.G. Jung: The First Complete English Edition of the Works of C.G. Jung*, Routledge, 1973

Carl Jung, *Memories, Dreams, Reflections*, Pantheon Books, 1963

Clarissa Pinkola Estés, *Women Who Run With the Wolves: Myths and Stories of the Wild Woman Archetype*, Ballantine Books, 1992

Elizabeth Alvilda Petroff, *Body & Soul: Essays on Medieval Women and Mysticism*, 1994

Amber Tamblyn's many, many diaries.